Whispers in the Wilderness

Whispers in the Wilderness

Finding Treasures of the Heart

Judy Leighton

To order additional copies of this book, contact:

Xlibris Corporation

1-888-795-4274

www.Xlibris.com

Orders@Xlibris.com

15085

CONTENTS

Dedication

To my dearest husband, my son and daughter,
parents, relatives and friends.

Because of my husband's devoted love for me shining through his many hours
of working with me editing and contributing to my two books, as well as the
loving support of my son and daughter, we give this true love story to you.

Whispers in a Wilderness

Whispering peace, reflections winging love returning to see
Grace healing, finding joy—each other, dawning hearts free

Compassion, abysmal pain and 'false light' within our pasts
Why so blindingly, we could not see to be, now see at last

Forgiving, unknowingly lack knowing, innocent emptiness
Bridging chasms, calmly crossing thru emerald wilderness

Glowing, radiant sunshine, illumined grace and love appear
Misting confusion of doubts, fear and pain virtuously clear

Always giving warmth, and vision, when we're unable to see
Perpetually understanding growing souls in crowning harmony

INTRODUCTION

WHISPERS IN THE WILDERNESS is an autobiographical self-help book well worth the read.

The book documents the personal path of Judy Leighton, Pain & Stress Consultant that led to the development of her method of inner healing. The Method addresses double binds (mental/emotional traps), and gives techniques that provide healthy alternatives in problem solving. Like every good life story, this one focuses on career, love, finding a soul mate, and destiny.

This text shares highly personal spiritual experiences, and how Judy receives hints of the future leading her on surprising paths. She highlights the positive impact of her self-help method of letting go of depression, fear, pain and suffering, and for defusing violence. She presents the method through the use of numerous clinical vignettes from her private consulting and weekly public seminars in medical facilities, as well as her own life experiences. The text is truly inspiring, offering hope, and therapeutic techniques to others suffering from various life traumas.

I have had the pleasure of knowing Judy for over thirty years. She is an empathic consultant, gifted musician, and lover of life. Her warmth and compassion for others is a gift she shares with the reader of this touching manuscript. Enjoy it!

David A. Baron, MSEd, D.O., DFAPA
(Distinguished Fellow American Psychiatric Association)
Assist. Dean, International Relations,
Keck School of Medicine, USC, Los Angeles
Professor and Vice Chair, Department of Psychiatry
Psychiatrist-in-Chief, Keck Medical Center at USC

FOREWORD

WHAT A WONDERFUL TESTIMONY of faith, hope, and trust—the virtues (i.e. strengths) that make the spirit within blossom and bear fruit. The author developed a method of inner healing for herself, and went on as a Pain & Stress Consultant in medical treatment centers giving this method to others. How was the author able to avoid the inherent danger involved in a creative act of writing wherein one relives the debilitating condition from which she liberated herself?

As I read her story, it is because she was able to recognize the miracle that happens when one lives in the moment with what comes one's way—doing what is healthy, creating health in unhealthy situations, and she discovered a simple method for releasing that which is unhealthy. This can be described as recognizing the "creativity of self" which affords one the opportunity to create one's own future. The willingness to do this is based on the recognition and acceptance of what is healthy for oneself. This is not a self centered selfishness, but a *healthy selfishness*. That is to say, we remain connected with everyone and everything around us, but we recognize and accept that if we do not take care of our self, we cannot take care of anyone else.

The psychologist, Rollo May, noted that a "dying" to part of one's self is often followed by a heightened awareness of life, a heightened sense of possibility. The author's message is clear:

"I let die that part of me that was destructive to me, and I am now living a new life with a vibrancy of awareness that has not only been heightened, but which enables me to make real the connectedness, the possibilities and dreams for which I longed." (My words)

In conclusion, I wish to note that this book is written from a female *and* male perspective. It reveals that there are more similarities between the sexes than differences. We are all from and on one planet and one plane. In the words of the British novelist, E.M. Forster, "We need only connect," with ourselves and with each other.

Reverend Francis J. Marcolongo,
S.T.L., S.S.L., Ph.D., MFT
Escondido, California

AUTHOR'S INTRODUCTION

My first book A Path to Light: How to Not Not Make Healthy Choices, documents my healing method. It addresses mental/emotional traps, including fear and pain from memories, and provides research footnotes. My method aids in more quickly letting go of fear, sadness, anger, and also may prevent violence. This book, Whispers in the Wilderness tells my surprising adventures as I searched for healing, and developed a healing process that unexpectedly worked quickly.

In 1965, when I was 21, I wanted to know how to get off the merry-go-round of the depression, fear, pain, guilt, and repetitive flashbacks that I had since childhood. Forgiving others was not an issue, and I began my search in therapy. At 40, I discovered how, after being diagnosed with a mixed-connective tissue disease and was facing death. My unique confrontation with death gave me the safety to ask a relevant question, and received an answer.

One evening before falling asleep, I asked, "What is missing from the minds of people who don't do what is best for themselves and others?" In the middle of the night, I was awakened with an answer. This assisted me to understand how other conflicting issues were related—interwoven, and see more answers on how to resolve them. With these answers, I developed a simple healing method ("A Dissociative Method to release Psychobiologic Binds"—"The Sunshine Method") to deal with my overwhelming emotional and physical fear and pain.

Using my method, surprisingly, just 10 days later my depression, together with my longstanding unnecessary fear, pain, guilt, and flashbacks had gone—disappearing permanently from my memories. I still had my factual memories, but without the pain associated with them.

My process includes new interpretations and perspectives in logic, and tools that I applied using language and logic to safely release myself. My inner work directly addressed some previously "hidden" interwoven and interlocked mental/emotional traps. These traps had created a false safety that was, in fact, hurtful, yet had helped me cope with past and present circumstances. A tangled web of traps had also prevented me from thinking of other alternatives. The result was what I call the "Circular Disposition Syndrome," which I was able to transform into new dispositions.

Release from these traps included addressing, resolving and then safely releasing some conflicts and old fear and pain. This was within my personal, collective subconscious, and unconscious, and within the realm of *spiritual issues* through a particular process. Part of the process is how to "safely" and immediately have a healthy self-worth, and how to be more constructive without the need for unnecessary fear and pain as a protective defense. This is a mental/emotional anti-depressant process—the "Sunshine Method," including a mental exercise program. I learned how to be safe in a new way, even while taking wise and healthy risks.

After doing this method for *two more weeks*, my physical pain also disappeared. The illness was in remission. Without belief or even the will to live, I had gained a high degree of inner peace. For me, this contributed to quickly transforming my mental and physical health. Because of this, I gained greater clarity, and was able to make many more wise and healthy choices. This included choosing a healthier balance. Retelling the story of the events from my past was not necessary to achieve this transformation.

One reason why my method worked so quickly is because I addressed and solved many interrelated mental/emotional issues at the same time. In my case, my balanced diet wasn't an issue. After becoming ill, because of physical pain I hadn't been able to write, play the piano, walk (only limp) or exercise. Also, I was allergic to anti-inflammatory drugs.

After healing, I wrote a short booklet about my experience, and was invited to present my simple method. It was a complicated task to *explain the concept of interwoven and interlocking traps, and how and why my simple method works.* In 1985, my method was recognized by psychiatrist Dr. David Baron, who became my consultant and later wrote the introduction for both of my books. In 1987 I began presenting my method as a Pain & Stress Consultant in medical treatment centers. Dr. Baron became the Deputy Director of the National Institute of Mental Health in Bethesda, MD (1987-92).

From Dr. Baron I learned that I had developed a healing method which included creating a form of cognitive restructuring with behavioral intervention that focuses on basic control issues.

My healing method may give you some added tools to release yourself and heal. The process begins by focusing on some new messages found in my Emergency Work Sheet, and using my Self-Worth Exercise for discovery and release exercises (in the Appendix). Instead of reinforcing the old mental/emotional traps, addressing these old problems in a unique way (often enough) may allow you to "safely" let them go. Through untying the knots of nots, and this new form of disuse, old painful feelings may disappear (also mentioned in my book, *A Path to Light: How to Not Not Make Healthy Choices*).

This is done by using some similar and different words, creating new different overlapping constructive thoughts. The process is like a train switching tracks at a junction and then traveling on a new track with new interpretations and language. The baggage of your painful feelings or numbness may be left behind on the old track, and may disappear like a path that is no longer used. I still retained my memories, but without the unnecessary painful emotions associated with them. Also, I had new constructive feelings appear, along with some formerly repressed positive feelings.

With greater clarity, I'm better able to know what I want to do in life, and how to participate in creating a more constructive future. For me, there were also many unexpected connecting events that occurred (sometimes thousands of miles away), that were seemingly beyond my conscious knowledge, intuition and creation. Many of these are mentioned in this book. One such exciting event is how at the age of 53, I mysteriously met my soul mate in a most unusual setting under extraordinary circumstances. Some of my poetry, written many years earlier, is included, which seems to have been a herald of my future—a healing method, and finding my soul mate to aid me in sharing with others. Some of my experiences just seem beyond the beyond.

As a consultant for doctors in medical treatment centers, I presented my healing method privately and in weekly group public seminars to people with cancer, arthritis, other chronic illness, physical pain, depression, addictions, and problems in everyday life. The Healing Kit, found in the Appendix, includes an Emergency Work Sheet, etc., which was also included in my first book, *A Path to Light.*

You may be unknowingly using an illusory form of protection (obeying a destructive 'self-protection' program), or just doing it out of habit. This explains why you may be continuing your unnecessary hurtful thinking and behavior even after knowledge and/or punishment. Also this may explain why many of you may have had difficulty making wise and healthy choices even when you knew better.

You may be aware of your unnecessary fear, guilt, anger, sadness, and flashbacks, or you may be gutsing/charging through life with your feelings stored safely below your level of awareness. Either way, my method may give you a safe way to deal with those feelings to gain your release. Also, you may gain confidence that you can deal with whatever problems you are facing, which may even include assistance from others.

Being in a greater state of harmony through this healing method, may provide you a "safe" new way to *"feel and be safe with healthy comfort and safety."*

Creating new healthy thought and behavior patterns does require using the tool of discipline. When you may lapse, just begin again. Healthy nutrition, which may include taking supplements and daily exercise (when possible) may contribute to your well being. Also, intermittent movement throughout each day, safe adequate sunlight and natural hormone replacement may be other factors in healing. Research studies demonstrate that relaxation and exercise programs benefit general health (pp. 117-118).

After healing, you may continue focusing on and using the messages of this method which may aid you in maintaining your healing, and further strengthening yourself.

In today's fast-paced world with so much tension, sadness, anger, and violence, there are times when you may feel overwhelmed with conflicting information and confusion. This simple healing method may be vital for quickly releasing unnecessary barriers, confusion, and pain—to be safe with safety. This aids in greater clarity and confidence to make many more wise choices and *stick with them*. Also, my healing method can be compatible with other methods and beliefs.

Meaningful, productive lives and healthy relationships can reach beyond ourselves to affect our human family and our environment—ultimately "creating and radiating greater dignity, peace and harmony" for everyone.

Judy Leighton,
Pain & Stress Consultant

If you want to jump in and begin your healing process, you may skip to the Appendix, read, and do the exercises in the "Prevention and Healing Kit." If problems with your appetite, you can focus on the messages there. To learn more about my healing method, read Ch. 17. Path to Discovery. Ch. 4. Mysterious Gifts, pp. 73-74, has details on focusing on a pulse to aid relaxation. To follow the tale of my adventures, naturally, begin at the beginning.

ACKNOWLEDGMENTS

M Y FATHER AND MOTHER who gave me love, and the childhood experiences of living in Japan from 1948-51, and then Germany from 1953-56, as well as travel to many other countries and states in the United States. This made it possible for me to experience the universal oneness of us all, and that there are kind, loving, and constructive people everywhere. I'm very grateful to my sister, grandparents, many relatives, and many friends for their love and encouragement. Also, thank you to my son, and to my daughter, a Mental Health Counselor, for the rewarding times we had editing the book jackets, and my Author Introduction.

To Dr. David Baron, psychiatrist, who made it possible for me to be a guest consultant in medical treatment centers. Since 1987, he has given continuous support and valuable suggestions as a consultant, reviewing this book, and involved in the editing of the Introduction on my cassette tapes and CD's. Dr. Baron was the Deputy Director of the National Institute of Mental Health in Bethesda, Md., Medical Director and Psychiatrist-in-Chief of Kirkbride Center, in Philadelphia, PA, and Professor and Chair, Department of Psychiatry and Behavioral Science, Temple University School of Medicine, PA. Presently, Dr. Baron is Asst. Dean, International Relations, Keck School of Medicine at USC, Los Angeles, Professor and Vice Chair, Department of Psychiatry, Psychiatrist-in-Chief, Keck Medical Center, Director, Global Center for Exercise, Psychiatry and Sports at USC.

To Patti Baron, mother, sports coach, and coordinator for a large community youth soccer program, a retired Teacher, and High School Varsity Tennis Coach for the past 6 years. She gave me valuable suggestions in editing this book, and reviewed the Introduction of my Young People's CD. The Introduction gives instructions to parents for their children and young people on how to use my method and CD.

To Francis Marcolongo, PhD., MFC, STL, SSL, a multi-lingual scholar who, as a family therapist, uses theology as part of the healing process. He was the Vice-President and Treasurer, of my Non-profit Foundation, and was involved in the editing of the Introduction on my cassette tapes, and this manuscript.

To Donna Davis Marcolongo, mother, real estate agent, involved in community service, who gave us valuable support for our project.

To Barbara McWilliams, former Secretary of my Non-profit Foundation, who also provided valuable editing suggestions for this book.

To Glen (Mac) McWilliams, retired Deputy Sheriff, and Police Officer, in 1989, recipient of award by Center Against Sexual Abuse (CASA). My thanks for his contributions to our project for the prevention of domestic violence.

To Maxwell Sanford Miller, attorney, in Marina Del Rey, who in addition to donating much of his time protecting my creative work, gave me valuable suggestions in written communication.

To the hundreds of individuals I taught how to use this healing method. Because of their participation, courage to do this method, and their results, there is increased evidence to support that the method in this book gives people tools to use to make life better for themselves and others.

To the following people who gave permission for our conversations to be published:

Dr. Arturo Gonzalez, psychiatrist, Tampa, Florida, for suggesting R.D. Laing's book *Knots*.

Dr. George Solomon, M.D., psychiatrist, Professor of Psychiatry at the University of California at Los Angeles (UCLA), formerly at VA Medical Center, in San Fernando Valley, Ca.

George LeDoux Ph.D., professor at the Center for Neural Science at New York University, and author.

Anthony Walsh, Ph.D., professor of Anthropology, Criminology and Sociology in the Department of Criminal Justice at Boise State University, Idaho, and author, for his suggestions for my early manuscript.

F. David Peat, Ph.D, physicist, author, Italy, for reviewing my manuscript.

To my friend and advisor, Joan DiFabio, a certified appraiser in Philadelphia, who graciously shared her home and daily drove me to a psychiatric hospital while I was a consultant there.

To all the educators, innovators, researchers and health professionals of anthropology, medicine, psychiatry, psychology, neurophysiology, religion, history and philosophy as well as self-help books that shared their ideas and gave me hope.

1. MYSTERY OF THE FLEUR-DE-LIS PIN

ONE CLEAR STARLIT EVENING, standing at the edge of what seemed to be the end of the earth, on the warm sandy beach, facing the Atlantic Ocean, I was 19 years old. The night was aglow with constellations seeming to give messages. Wondering, I asked, "Who and where are you?"—thinking of the love of my life I had yet to meet, and what will my future career be?

In the early 60's, for less than two years I worked for the government. In that brief window in time, I experienced an unexpected adventure. Very soon after I began working, we, the stenographers (4 of us), were given a tour of Cape Canaveral. After we settled into our hotel room, and had dinner that evening, I wandered down to the oceanfront by myself. Enjoying the beautiful starry night, I felt lonely, and wished I had someone special to share this wonderful evening.

The next afternoon at our hotel, we walked by the swimming pool, and unexpectedly our NASA guide introduced us to some of the first Astronauts—"Gus" Grissom, Walter Schirra, Alan Shepard, Scott Carpenter, Donald Slayton, John Young and one other. They were staying at our same hotel. On a lovely afternoon, we enjoyed talking with these charming men out by the swimming pool, and our pictures were taken with them.

There I was—just the night before asking the universe, "Where is the love of my life I had yet to meet?" and just hours later, amazingly, the universe paraded the select pick of the *supermen* of the era in front of us—in bathing suits, no less!

No, he was not one of them—they were all married! However, there was a hidden clue that unfolded years later—a connection with the Mercury Space Capsule design.

Another hidden clue to eventually finding my soul mate had been revealed many years before. Willed to me when I was 17 years old from my great-grandmother was a mysterious curiosity. When she passed away, she left me a piece of jewelry, a tiny solid-gold Fleur-de-lis (French lily flower) collar pin. She seemed to have no French background herself. I wondered what significance this pin may have for my life. Why did she have this pin, where and how did she get it?

When I was very young, I lovingly remember staying overnight with her in her two-story house. Her avocado trees were known for having the largest avocados in the area. We spent some happy evenings in her living room with the old-fashioned carpet where we danced with her dog, Blackie to the music on the radio. There was her bedroom with the old-fashioned dressing table in a dark musty corner, lined with colored perfume bottles. Sitting on her four-poster bed, we looked through the lacy leaves of the trees dancing with the sunshine. Breezy warm sunny days we sat together on her porch swings, along with my grandmother, mother, father and other relatives where we snapped beans and peeled and ate grapefruit. We would also travel together to a river and go fishing.

Another clue is that in my home I have some prints of Monet and Renoir's art. When one of my friends was studying art in France, he visited Monet's garden, and while there made a beautiful pastel of Monet's famous water lilies for me—a connection with the fleur-de-lis lily pin.

Of course, when I was 17, I had no idea that I had many challenges to face, knowledge to gain, and skills to develop to solve some puzzles before I would be led to my soul mate. Because my father was in the military, we had moved often during my childhood until I was 14. My parents faced an uncertain world and many stresses of being uprooted, having to live in two countries that had formerly been the enemy, in addition to being new young parents. They did their very best to make life better for my sister and me. In Germany, we were fortunate to live off the military base in a little farming town for approximately 1 year. There, we had the opportunity to make friends, and learn their language and customs.

Even though I gained some wonderful experiences and knowledge of people and other cultures, I missed a solid education and long-term connections with people. I knew very little about the world even though as a child, I had lived in several places in the United States, and in Japan in 1948-50 and Germany in 1953-56, as well as traveled to many other European countries. Being the eldest, as my sister, born in Germany, was 8 years younger than me, I didn't have the benefit of learning about the world from an older sibling.

Many of you, like myself, when we were children and later as adults sometimes experienced repeated pain and trauma, whether real, misunderstood or imagined, in everyday living situations. Sometimes this happened when left with baby-sitters, in school situations, at work, or whenever we felt alone and unprotected.

As long as I could, I read fairy tales, a few children's books, and bible stories to try and comfort myself, as well as looked for comfort in my religious upbringing.

Unresolved Fear, Pain and Guilt

To deal with my unresolved painful feelings from my childhood and youth, I first had to overcome my desire to *not* want to know much. Because of unknown barriers, I had been unable to be curious enough to actively seek knowledge that could be helpful. Later, at 21 I did have at least a little curiosity to want to know how to *let go* of the unnecessary depression, fear, pain, sadness, and guilt from my past, present and fear of the future.

When I asked a therapist how, he said that I needed to find the answers within myself, and to express my feelings. I didn't even know where or how to begin to find the answers within myself. I then asked him a very bizarre question: "When will I want to know something? I don't seem to want to know anything. I seem to have no curiosity." This just shows how confused I was because, at that time I did not even realize that I had just asked a question. He did say that one day my curiosity would turn on, just like a light switch.

My fleur-de-lis lily pin was forgotten, and soon I married someone who was an officer in the military, a life familiar to me. Later I gave birth to our two children, 2 1/2 years apart.

For five years I did my best to find the answers from others and within myself, and my curiosity came up against a blank wall. In looking back, an added difficulty that may have contributed to my blankness was my limited ability with language, which is discussed later. Curiosity is one of the factors that eventually led me to safety and continues to do so. However, it was necessary that in addition to improving my reading and language skills, I needed to be exposed to different perspectives related to my problem, which happened through reading and talking with people.

Along with continuing to pray everyday, I began Yoga exercises to see whether I could end my flashbacks. I enjoyed the physical exercises, and was very successful in gaining self-discipline. During meditation, I would focus on seeing white light. Sometimes I had some brief comforting experiences in between times, although my flashbacks of fear and pain would return. Sometimes when I was out for a walk, riding my bicycle or driving my car, spontaneously a white light would surround me, and briefly I felt one with God and the universe giving me temporary peace and relief.

Extraordinarily, at the birth of both my son and daughter, two and a half years apart, bright white light covered all of us, and seemed to spread throughout the room. I felt the most unique beautiful feelings that I had never felt before or since.

Nevertheless, even with these powerful experiences, most of the time, I was still stuck with fear, pain, and guilt from memories, as well as present painful realities. Through doing yoga, I hadn't permanently relieved or solved this key problem. Then and until I was 40 years old, I was not aware that I was at the mercy of many tangled thoughts and misinterpretations (mental/emotional traps). I also didn't realize that my limited ability with language was also a barrier.

Because I had wanted to learn to play piano since I was a child, I thought now, while my two children are little, I would have the time to learn. We bought an antique oak upright piano with beautiful woodcarvings of wreaths. A Dentist was selling his piano because his teenagers didn't want to learn to play anymore, and had bought them a jukebox.

Two weeks later my husband called and said that his military orders had been changed, and we were all going to move to Hawaii. Soon after we moved to Hawaii when I was 26, I began piano lessons, and a year later began taking courses part-time at a Community College.

Reading Comprehension Problems

Because I had serious reading comprehension problems, the year before entering college my task became reading books written for the teenage level to develop my very limited reading and speaking skills.

In relation to books, my mother told me that when she was growing up, my grandmother loved to read so much that my mother felt ignored. When I was growing up there were hardly any books in our house. I had a Bible, a few Bobsey Twin books, and some fairy-tale books. Both my parents worked hard, and didn't have much time for reading, other than the newspaper. Later, when I was 15, we got a television, and it became more dominant in our home.

As my grandmother grew older, maybe since we seldom saw her because we lived out of the country and state, she *did* pay a lot of attention to us when we came to visit. She may have still been reading a lot, but I didn't see her reading. I do have many happy memories though of just being with my grandmother and grandfather. We lived with my grandparents for a short time when I was young, and later, I did for a short time after I graduated from high school.

My mother did very well working in my grandfather's builder's supply company. When I was young, I worked there some summers, and enjoyed my grandfather riding me around on a forklift. Later, after my grandfather's company closed, my mother went on being successful working in other building supply companies. My sister is also a success in her own business. We all only have so much time each day to devote to the development of different skills, and I am very grateful for all I have been able to learn, even though late.

Beginning Solutions in the Library

To solve my reading comprehension problem, I went to the Honolulu library and found biographies and diaries written at the teenage level that I could handle. I thought these might be easier for me to read with understanding and comprehension. Also, they would be interesting and helpful to read about how other people thought, felt, talked, and what they did. Around this time, I began to have unusual experiences of receiving hints about the future, some of which later came true! Because of these experiences, I became more open to this unknown spiritual area.

The next year, starting college at 27, while my children were very young, I entered part-time as a piano major after only one year of piano. I still had language problems to deal with, as well as my intrusive painful thoughts and feelings. All this was very demanding. Even though my private reading was enjoyable, and I gradually improved my reading, it wasn't until much later that I was able to read with adequate comprehension. To get through college, I had to memorize, and it was tedious, and time-consuming, along with all my piano work. My husband and I lacked the knowledge and experience to balance our lives, and solve some complex problems. We grew apart, and later divorced. I continued with my education.

Since I wanted my children to love learning and reading, when they were elementary age, even though I had very little money, I put them in a school in Hawaii, called Hale Mohala (House of the Opening Blossoms). It was patterned after Summerhill, an alternative school in England. I had heard about it in my Philosophy class, and the very next day I went there to visit. The school was right next to the University of Hawaii. There were 5 teachers for 50 students, and it was for grades 1-6. Both my son and daughter have wonderful memories of their learning experience there, and love to learn and read. Because the school was close to where I was attending my courses at the University of Hawaii, on a few occasions, I was able to take them to some of my interesting classes.

One day I took them to my astronomy class, which had several hundred students. The professor asked two questions:

1. What is the subatomic makeup of the hydrogen atom? and
2. How many protons, electrons, neutrons are in a carbon atom?

My son, who was about 9 years old at the time, was the only one to raise his hand with the answers, which turned out to be correct. I was as surprised as everyone else. Another time, I went to get my daughter after school, and she was lying on the floor in the school library completely absorbed in a book. When she was 7, she was reading at the 7th grade level. Because of moving to another state, when they were 9 and 11, they then went to a public school and did very well.

Releasing Unnecessary Fear, Pain, and Guilt

When I was 40, I married again. Within the year after a returning from a science meeting in Europe, I became very ill with a rapid-moving mixed-connective-tissue disease that appeared hopeless and maybe fatal. Over an eight-month period my symptoms quickly worsened. I couldn't walk, drive, play piano or write my name, and I wanted to die. Because my husband was a scientist in the medical profession, I saw the best doctors available with access to the latest research at NIH. I wondered whether the continuous repetitive flashbacks of fear and pain from my past experiences were adversely affecting my immune system.

Facing death at 40, I desperately wanted to discover *how to let go* of my depression, fear, pain, sadness, and guilt so I could at least die in peace. I faced the reality that in my search since 21, I had not discovered from myself, other people or books how to permanently let go of my fear and pain from the past.

Next, I had to figure out by myself if answers even existed. Through many years of collecting information, asking God and myself for answers, and using my intuition, I was fortunate to receive, discover and put together some answers that worked. Then I developed a cognitive program and a mental relaxation exercise using these ideas. To my surprise and great relief, just *10 days later*, the fear, pain, and guilt from my memories were gone, permanently. Two weeks later, unexpectedly I had a *sudden remission* of my disease. By accident, through making some simple logical deductions, asking some relevant questions, and discovering answers, I developed a healing method that worked for me, and later for others.

Even though I did learn more complex language and ideas, actually, when ill and facing death, life had become more simple for me—*simple* to discover a *simple preventive and healing method*. At that time, I was only trying to heal my mental/emotional pain just so I could die in peace.

My Background

In 1985, based on some discoveries then and from 1979, I developed an original stress-reduction methodology. In 1986, I wrote up my method to aid other people with chronic stress, panic disorders, and serious illness, and began sharing with others. My method was soon recognized by Dr. David Baron, Psychiatrist, who became my consultant.

Dr. Baron was the Deputy Director of the National Institute of Mental Health, Medical Director/Psychiatrist-in-Chief of Kirkbride Center, Philadelphia, and Professor and Chair, Department of Psychiatry at Temple University School of Medicine, Philadelphia.

Presently, Dr. Baron is Asst. Dean, International Relations, Keck School of Medicine at USC, Los Angeles, Professor and Vice Chair, Department of Psychiatry, and Psychiatrist-in-Chief, Keck Medical Center at USC.

From 1987-1996, I was a guest Pain and Stress Consultant at several medical treatment centers in the Los Angeles area, in 1989 established a Foundation, a non-profit corporation to present group seminars, and continue private consultations with individuals.

In 1987 I was a guest consultant in a health care clinic, in Inglewood, CA, and in 1988, began in another medical treatment center consulting for individuals and families. They had been diagnosed with cancer, and other chronic diseases.

In 1990, I began presenting weekly public seminars through my non-profit foundation at the Van Nuys Psychiatric Hospital, and later at other hospitals, community centers, and for a company that sponsored 12-step programs.

Many problems addressed were repetitive fear and pain from memories, panic attacks, attempted suicide, physical and sex abuse, weight-loss or gain, eating disorders, and addictions—smoking, drugs and alcohol—which all include gaining a healthy self-control and ending self-destructive behavior. Also, I was a consultant for young people who were handi-capable, with learning disabilities.

A variety of public and professional organizations invited me to speak and demonstrate my method. At an acute-care psychiatric hospital in the suburbs of Philadelphia, I demonstrated my method to medical students with acute in-patients. At a continuing education program for Chemical Dependency and other Addictions for a Hospital Community Education Program for nurses and doctors, I was invited to talk on spiritual blocks, as well as solutions for recovery. At Senior Retirement Home Centers and Senior Community Centers, I demonstrated how to more easily let go of the fear, pain and guilt from memories, and the other aspects of my healing method.

Additional communication tools I developed have aided people to more rapidly and effectively gain a healthy self-worth, confidence and self-control to de-fuse and/or resolve conflicts, as well as let go of destructiveness, and to make other wise, healthy choices to experience greater inner peace and joy. These tools are in the Appendix: Preventive and Healing Kit, also with a work sheet for those in an *emergency or too busy.*

Many years later, after healing and having more exposure to and understanding of more complex thought and language patterns through reading, I wrote a book on my healing method—*A Path to Light: How to Not Not Make Healthy Choices.* That book explains why this simple preventive and healing method works. The method is simple. Explaining *how and why* it works is more complex.

In looking back, because of earlier having such problems with speaking, reading, and writing, the combination of my gathering particular and diverse information, along with many years of memorizing music and playing the piano, made it easier for my brain to hold enough relevant information for the task. Then I had enough pieces of the puzzle to make a whole picture of some of the *"interwoven problems"* connected to fear, pain, and guilt.

Facing death allowed me to ask the appropriate questions and receive answers that worked, so that I *did* discover, before it was too late, how to let go of unnecessary depression, fear, pain, sadness, and guilt quickly and easily. Then, unexpectedly, instead of dying, I soon healed and learned how to live in peace. Next, from 1987 to 1996, I presented this healing method at various hospitals and medical treatment centers, and began writing a book about the healing method. Having learned to live in peace and to appreciate life more completely than I had ever known, I wanted to live more simply, and then was led to my soul mate in a most unexpected exciting way—a real-life adventure!

Finding My Soul Mate

My question as to where is my soul mate wasn't answered until after a long search—I was 53 and he 71. I don't know whether we could have found each other any sooner. Our experiences are a great mystery—a real life dream come true. Many of you, like I, have had some wonderful spiritual moments and synchronistic experiences with potential intimate relationships in the past. Maybe there was not enough compatibility to lead to a lasting bond with someone, or perhaps, the bond was broken through negative attitudes and behavior. In sharing our story, maybe you can find your soul mate sooner, or recognize the one you may already have.

Some people have suggested that when you want to meet your love to write down on a piece of paper what you want in a mate, including many details such as profession, money, looks, education, hobbies, etc. My list was very simple. I focused on "I am always safe meeting the compatible love of my life, with mutual respect, compassion, trust, love, affection, harmony and joy. Also, this person honors the healing method I developed, my son, and daughter, and myself. This is important because I have the responsibility of sharing this healing method with people through books and talks. This person needs to understand the healing method, and through using it also be healed.

The magic carpet did not fly in with him. Over many years, I met a number of men who were good people, yet did not meet these criteria. I did not think the words "SOUL MATE." I always had used the words "the Love of my Life." Also, some friends told me that because I was so preoccupied with writing my book, I probably wouldn't meet this person until my book was published. Maybe their thoughts were interfering. I hoped and prayed that I would meet him sooner.

In 1976, I wrote the following poem in Hawaii which seems to have clues to my future.

From Death to Life

Wandering meadows, into forests unknown I went
Following path, seeing my healing cup was content
Listening, leaving happily my cup to share
Finding a key, opening, bringing me to where

Clearing, fog lifting, revealing gently, a lake I see
Drifting in, rippling open, warmth surrounded me
Remembering the warmth, seeing the wall
Climbing, sitting there, wondering about all

Going back to where I received the key
Giving to others—grace given to me
Hearing the spring, sharing leads me to sing
Healing others, knowing peace loving brings

Traveling again, finding my cup of love
Running over forever, flowing from above
Walking to the lake, hearing silently your call
Knowing you are waiting for me through it all

Finding you there, revealing the way I see
Waiting me for you, simply trusting we be
Receiving, giving grace, a way for you and me
Flowing through death into Life, we are free

(Written 1976)

2. MIDDLE OF NOWHERE EVERYWHERE?

FROM 1987 UNTIL 1996, I was traveling from the mountains many hours each week to a medical treatment center in Los Angeles consulting for many people with cancer and other diseases. This was very rewarding, however, this left little time and energy to complete writing my self-help book which could reach and aid so many more people. In the spring, I stopped my long commute and consulting, to stay in the mountains, and finish writing my book.

In November 1996, a secretary recommended me for the part-time job she was leaving. The job was to work for the owner of a company who needed someone to stay in his mansion, do some typing, and take care of his dogs and cats while he was away. This would give me more free time to concentrate on writing my book. At that time he was negotiating to buy another mansion on five acres of land, and wanted me to move there. After I had already given notice to leave my home, he discovered that his new property was not going to go through escrow in time.

In early December, he called, and said that his company already owned another property on 120 acres. He was also hiring a full-time caretaker and his wife to live there in one of the houses. On a beautiful sunny warm December day, he drove me into the wilderness to a ranch to see whether I would be willing to live there. As we were walking around the property, tears came to my eyes. This was one of the most beautiful, spiritual places I had ever seen. There were lakes, waterfalls, trees of many varieties and meadows sparkling in the sun, with warm sweet aromas scenting the air.

A week later I drove a friend of mine there for her to see this magnificent place. While we were there, we picked up some beautiful rocks. The one I picked up was a beautiful white crystal in the shape of a "heart" with pink lines running through it. Immediately, I thought, "Maybe I'll find my love out here." I began carrying this crystal with me everywhere.

In late December, with the help of my son and friends, I moved into the wilderness, and 9 deer were there to greet us. There I was in 1996 living out in what usually people have referred to as living in the "middle of nowhere." This large expanse of land I call "living in the middle of everywhere" because for me the forest and mountains are a place of many beautiful treasures and many forest paths that I could explore.

On over 100 acres, surrounded by other larger pieces of land and a National Forest, I was busy completing my first book on a prevention and healing method, "A Path to Light." The weather was sunny with crystal clear blue skies, and I had a wide expansive view of the valleys and mountains. I could see for miles. I felt joyfully inspired with so much greater freedom and a widening view to finally write the last chapter, which turned into two.

My companions were a couple of friends by telephone, two dogs, two cats, nine deer that would stand and talk with me, and a lion I only knew through his footprints in the sand. Daily, I wandered through a portal of overhanging trees into a magical meadow filled with butterflies. Passing through dancing wild flowers with soft breezes, floating puffy clouds above, the glittering leaves in the trees, climbing the mountains, and walking by the lakes, I was filled with joy. I feel I was given this inspiring place to complete my book. This is the most isolated I have ever lived. Also, this is the most breathtakingly beautiful, romantic place I have ever lived, and at the time no love to share this joyful place. I had lived in Los Angeles as well as in the mountains, and had not found my soul mate. I hoped he, in addition to being kind, would also have a background in physics. However, I was not near a university, so I questioned how? where? when? Is he ready to meet me? Does a soul mate for me even exist? (Later I explain why "Physics"?).

In January, I once walked up a different path into the forest while I was looking for my lost cat. She had been frightened the day she was first moved out here and had run away. Searching for my cat, I passed in sight of one of the few houses out there, just as the first snow was falling. Looking at the seemingly empty house, I wondered whether whoever owns this place will lead me to my love one day.

Several feet of snow fell. Fortunately my cat survived the snow blizzard and came back several days later. The blizzard had sent everyone else away, and then she felt safe to venture back to me. I didn't walk on that path for months—instead, I was cross-country skiing across our apple orchard while my two dogs were leaping through the snow like popcorn.

The Willow Lake

One day in April, I returned to that seldom-used path and walked farther, deeper into the forest. The enchanting path drew me winding up a lovely glade, with scents of sunlit grasses traveling the softened air, leading me to a beautiful small lake with a willow tree—draped weeping branches embracing gentle breezes—capturing a reflection of perfect peace caressing my soul with pads of white lilies on the water, surrounding lacy alder trees, all Springly arrayed, whispering breezes, preparing me unaware. So inspired by this beautiful place, I took a photograph to use for the cover of my book.

Walking further up into a meadow I saw many joyful daffodils waving in the breeze. I wondered who could have planted these?

Also that April I had another wonderful spiritual experience back on the other side of this sparkling forest—the path I usually walked twice a day. One day in late April, when I awakened in the morning, I felt very sad and lonely. Maybe I was feeling exhausted. Just a few days before, I had given my son his 30th birthday party over the previous weekend, which was such a wonderful, joyful experience. We had had a camp-out, and he had invited what he said was almost the whole village.

As I was saying, I felt so sad and lonely, and I had an appointment to get my hair cut at 1:00 PM. All of a sudden I had a strong feeling around 9 AM to call and cancel my appointment, and go for an extra long hike after lunch high into the mountains so I would feel better. I felt very embarrassed and argued with myself, but finally called and canceled anyway.

After lunch I left with my two dogs on our intended extra long hike into the high mountains. About 45 min. into our hike, the dogs wandered over to a big rock that was shaded by trees and began barking. I heard rustling, and didn't know whether there was a person or an animal behind the rocks. I felt very uncomfortable, and something told me to go back home immediately.

When I arrived home there was a message on my answering machine from a friend who said she needed help right away. Her young grandchild in a nearby State had called. She wanted to fly here today to see her grandmother. It was an emergency! We had not seen her in several years. We needed to be at the Ontario airport in another city by 5 PM. I knew we could just make it if I got ready right away, and went to pick up my friend. Arriving at the airport just in time with only a few minutes until the plane landed, we enjoyed the excitement.

When her granddaughter got off the airplane, she began telling us her story. She had felt very sad and lonely while packing her suitcase in the early morning. That was when I, too, had felt sad and lonely, and had called and canceled my hair appointment not knowing why. There were serious problems, and she had felt an urgency to come and be with her grandmother. We had a joyous time together, and sang all the way home.

A few days later they visited me. I took them for a walk in the special forest where days before I had heard rustling in the bushes, and felt I should return home immediately. It was then that I unexpectedly found her grandmother's urgent phone message.

Again, I marveled at how spiritual circumstances had often brought me together with others even though I was hidden in a remote area. There I was having another special experience like many of the other special spiritual experiences in my life, so where is my soul mate? Did he even exist?

Since God had given me many wonderful experiences to share with people, why hadn't God brought me my soul mate? My list and prayer describing my soul mate was "I am now meeting a kind man who honors the healing method, my son, daughter, and me—also a background in physics would be helpful" (explained later).

Maybe one of the reasons I didn't meet my soul mate any sooner was because I rarely had been able to make the necessary time to focus on him. My full energy was being used commuting long distances presenting in a medical treatment center, and seminars in hospitals. Also, I was developing cassette tapes, writing up studies and research reports, reviewing research papers and books, and writing my book.

On April 6, I had completed the last chapter that was being readied for peer review. On July 11, I had finished my revisions on the whole manuscript and mailed it to an agent. Finally, I could relax! The property was changing ownership, and the caretaker and his wife were preparing to leave. Even though I had been given the option to stay, and the isolation had been ideal for finishing the manuscript, I missed my friends and thought I'd move back to the village. I began to search for a house there. Very soon, with my attention relieved from the manuscript, I felt the emptiness of not having a real soul mate.

The night of August 13, 1997, my loneliness reached to despair. I then had an emergency talk with God. "You know the men that have been coming into my life are not my soul mate. I don't know where or when to find him. If you know where he is, please bring him to me. I have done all you have asked of me. I consulted for, and shared the healing method with many children and adults that may to save their relationships and marriages, consulted in medical treatment centers and hospitals for people having chronic stress and diseases, taught public seminars and completed the manuscript. If you do not bring him to me, I don't feel that I can go on with this work. I feel too lonely and cannot go on without my soul mate. I was hoping that maybe I could just disappear into thin air, and I fell asleep crying.

The next morning I felt so much better and renewed my commitment to continue sharing the healing method with others even though I didn't have my soul mate. I also thought that I am going to talk and listen to God more often—even when I do feel lonely. Maybe there isn't a soul mate for me. After my early morning walk in the sparkling forest, I left for my work in the village.

Throughout the day I reminisced about other happy adventures that God and the Angels had led me on through the years. Some of these adventures are told in the following chapters. Little did I know that the night before, the spiritual forces beyond had also gone to work, as at times they had unexpectedly done in the past.

Lost is a Place Too

Lost is a place too
Dawning insights, life renews
Knowing your way through
Life sparkles anew
Feel compassion, feel love
Feel grace from above
Now I am here with you
Lost in a Universe, we, too

Lost is a place too
Finding how is where you
Release your fear, letting go pain
Seeing inside, feeling the gain
Safely to love, peace softly falls
Miracles descending now to all
Receiving, giving, being with you
Lost together our souls renew

(Title written 1976, poem 1986)

3. CRYSTAL BELLS

WHEN I WAS 25 years old, the whispering thought came to me that I would start taking piano lessons and become a concert pianist. I had wanted to play the piano since I was 6 years old, but my parents couldn't afford to provide me with lessons. Also, because of having learning disabilities, I don't know whether I would have been able to learn very well anyway. I had been unable to read with very much comprehension, and had resorted to memorizing as my only way of learning. Also, I was unable to speak very much. Music was to become my language through gifted teachers.

At 26 I began piano lessons with a lady, who was a graduate of the Juilliard School of Music. At the same time I began getting books (mostly biographies) from the children's section in the Honolulu Public Library with the hope of learning to read with comprehension. After one year of piano lessons, with the hard work of memorizing and intense dedication, I realized that I had also missed a childhood learning experience with children's music. I called the nearby Community College, and inquired whether they had a course teaching piano music with musical games for children. They said that there was no such course, and invited me to audition as a piano performance major. I auditioned, was accepted, and studied with a very talented piano professor there.

Several years later, following another audition, I transferred to the University of Hawaii majoring in piano performance. I studied with Professor Peter Coraggio, a graduate of Juilliard, and author of many piano instruction books.*

Goals and Attitudes

There were several other people whose suggestions aided me in eventually reaching my goal to perform with an orchestra, and my continued search for how to let go of depression, fear and pain from memories. One of them was Reverend Doug Olson, a Clinical Pastoral Counselor, where I went to church at Calvary By The Sea in Honolulu, Hawaii. He told me that some people have been stuck in the habit of pain. He also said that some people feel safer with strangers in the beginning, and unsafe with people who are familiar. This is because of their past experiences of pain with familiar people. He told me that I really was safe now, although at the time, I was so lost in my repetitive flashbacks of fear and pain that I was unable to absorb completely and use what he was saying. The thoughts were seeds being planted that eventually flowered.

He also told me the story of how the great ballet dancer Nureyev, who started quite late to learn to dance, had set his goal: He said, "I am a dancer," (rather than I am going to be a dancer) as he started the long work to become a professional. I began saying (only to myself), "I am a concert pianist," as I started my training. This focus was partially instrumental in my being led to a concert pianist, Bernardo Segall in Los Angeles, but in a most unexpected spiritual way.

Reverend Doug Olson and his wife Ivy both contributed encouragement and support for my reaching my goals in piano with grace, love and support for my children and me when I was having a difficult time. While rehearsing by myself in our church, a surprising spiritual mystery related to my future piano career began. In addition to the thought processes that they both shared with me, they got me an opportunity to use a piano for study in another church in a retirement home in Waikiki. There unexpectedly I met a concert pianist who had recently moved to Hawaii, and had just wandered in looking for a piano, just moments after I had begun playing. The rest of this story is told later. Doug and Ivy continued in their mission of aiding others and the homeless through the Angel Network, which Ivy founded in 1989.

Visualization

After a few years of study at the university, I changed from studying with my piano professor, and embarked on a new adventure. While I continued all my other music studies at the university, I went to study piano privately with a woman named Ellen Masaki, alumna of University of Hawaii, and the Manhattan School of Music, and one of the leading trainers of child prodigies in Hawaii. I was curious about how she taught, how the children learned, and what had I missed by not learning in childhood.

Another of my beginning experiences of being in a wonderful place at just the right time came as a result. A few weeks after just beginning to study with her, I went to my lesson one day, and she came running out to meet me at the gate. She asked, "Guess who is here?" I had no idea. She said Vladimir Ashkenazy. Just the day before, I had been in the concert hall, hearing him perform with the Honolulu Symphony orchestra in front of thousands of people in the audience.

Ellen led me around her house in the back way to her kitchen, and we sat and listened to him rehearsing. Eventually, he stopped and came to greet us. Vladimir invited Ellen and gave her free tickets so she could bring two of her students to his next concert on Maui. Ellen invited one of her other students and me. A week or two later we were there attending his concert, and our pictures were taken with Vladimir and his wife at the reception. I thought I was in a fairy-tale.

In addition to Ellen sharing her wonderful teaching techniques, she loaned me a cassette tape by Dr. Carl Simonton, well known for his visualization work with cancer patients. She shared the tape with me for the purpose of part of my piano instruction. I had no idea then that one day I would be presenting my future healing method to people with cancer and other diseases.

Ellen asked me to visualize myself performing in a concert successfully. This was very beneficial even though I couldn't visualize an image. I did use my imagination, pretending and using my thought processes since I am more sound-oriented. She also gave me many wonderful enriching experiences of meeting and learning ideas from well-known concert pianists in her home. We also attended master classes and concerts with performers Vladimir Ashkenazy, Lorin Hollander, etc.

In March 2000, Ellen was honored and given the Music Teacher of the Year 2000 award by the Music Teacher's National Association in Minneapolis, Minnesota. This is the first time in its 124-year history that they have given this award.

Spiritual Guidance

Less than a year after I began study with Ellen, one day I was rehearsing in the church Calvary By The Sea. A surprising whispering message came floating through my thoughts and said, "Someone is coming to lead you to a master concert pianist connected to Rachmaninov somewhere on the mainland United States." I thought, "Why me? Is this wishful thinking?"

An opportunity had been offered to me by Reverend Doug Olson to use a piano in the sanctuary of another church in Waikiki for rehearsing. Recovering from the flu, I went to that church a few weeks earlier than we agreed, hoping I would get inspired and heal faster. The church was the entire 12th floor of a condominium, which is a retirement home for the Lutheran Church in Waikiki. There were large glass windows overlooking the ocean on one side, and overlooking the velvet green mountains on the other side. The sanctuary is called the "Prince of Peace." I was there a short time struggling to play as I was very weak from the flu.

Quietly, a young man walked in and sat down in the back of the church. I thought he had come to pray. Very soon he came forward and asked me with whom I was studying. I told him Ellen Masaki. He then said, "What a coincidence! I am a concert pianist from Bolivia, I've recently married and moved here from Los Angeles with my wife. Just today, I signed a contract to teach for your teacher." Immediately I thought, "This is the one I am looking for." I jokingly asked, "What took you so long? I've been waiting all my life for you."

This sounded so strange coming from myself, because this young man and his wife had just moved to Hawaii, so there was no reason to think he would be leaving anytime soon. I thought this was quite the mark of destiny. Here I was in this church two weeks before I was supposed to be, and the message I had been given through my thoughts a month earlier in my other church was beginning to unfold—"Someone is coming to lead you to a master concert pianist on the mainland."

When I went to my next lesson, I asked my teacher, Ellen, if she would release me from my contract with her, so I could study with this new concert pianist. This would put me in the background, so I would not feel pressure to perform yet. She kindly released me, and I began my studies with him.

At first my new teacher said he would be in Hawaii five years. It made sense to me that in five years I would have attained that degree of technical and musical expertise needed to be accepted as a student by an eminent piano master. Seven months later, he came to my lesson, and said that he was returning to Los Angeles. He also said that I must go too, or I would never make it. Then he said that he would lead me to a master teacher. He left in February, and I left the following June when I finished my course work at the University of Hawaii.

Meeting the Master Teacher

The following Fall, I transferred to major in music at Cal State University, Los Angeles, and studied with him outside the university for another six months.

In December, as he had promised, he introduced me to Bernardo Segall, a world-renowned concert pianist, and soon I started a long program of study with him. Bernardo had studied with Rachmaninov's teacher and cousin, Alexander Siloti, who had been the conductor for the Imperial Orchestra in Russia. When the Czar was overthrown, Siloti went to New York and taught for the Juilliard School of Music.

When Bernardo was 14 years old, in San Paulo, Brazil, he won a piano competition and was given a scholarship to study with the master of his choice anywhere in the world. He had played for Arthur Rubenstein, and Rubenstein recommended that he study with Siloti in New York. Bernardo went with his mother to New York to meet and play for Siloti. He told him that he could stay and study with him.

He told me a humorous story that happened after one of the Sunday dinners. Siloti told Rachmaninov to play for the boy. He began the opening of his Second Piano Concerto, which Bernardo had never heard. At first Bernardo thought that Rachmaninov felt insulted to play for someone so young, and was making fun of him by playing the simple opening of the piano concerto. Very quickly Bernardo was relieved when the beautiful sounds of the concerto became more complex.

My earlier hint in Hawaii about being led to a master teacher connected to Rachmaninov had been fulfilled. Also interesting, is that when I began to study with Bernardo, I took him a Rachmaninov Prelude that I had been playing in Hawaii in the church at the time that the thought came to me that I would be led to meet a master teacher. I wanted to see if there was any special significance to the piece. We looked at the top of the page, and it was dedicated to Alexander Siloti, who I had not known was Bernardo's *own* master teacher. We were both amazed. When I was in Hawaii, I had never noticed the name, because I was such a novice and not very knowledgeable as to names in music. Many times a composition is dedicated to a patron. Bernardo trained me until years later I auditioned, and performed with the Los Angeles Doctors' Symphony Orchestra in April 1989 to raise money for charitable causes.

Thank you also to the many other aspects of this healing method, the support of my former husband, Bernardo's brilliant teaching techniques, and the wonderful instruction by the guest conductor Joel Lish, the talents of the Los Angeles Doctors' Symphony Orchestra, and 5 professional Choirs. We went on to accomplish what many might think was the impossible—since I had not even begun to learn to play the piano until I was 26 years old. Mr. Lish continues to be conductor of the Palisades Symphony Orchestra.

In 1988, I passed my audition with the Los Angeles Doctors' Symphony Orchestra, and through my non-profit foundation, organized a fundraising interfaith concert for chronic disease projects. In April 1989, as piano soloist with the Doctors' Symphony, we performed Beethoven's Choral Fantasie in Los Angeles. Dr. Baron, who at that time was Deputy Director of the National Institute of Mental Health, Bethesda, spoke at the concert about my projects as a Pain and Stress Consultant for people with chronic stress and disease.

Organizing and performing the concert was happening at the same time that I had a very busy schedule presenting my healing method to many individuals in crisis situations.

---

*   Coraggio, Peter, *The Art of Piano Performance*, (California, Neil A. Kjos Music Co., 2000).

4. MYSTERIOUS GIFTS

EARLY IN 1980, I had begun studying with concert pianist Bernardo Segall in Los Angeles, and in 1983 I married. My two teen-agers and I went to live in my husband's cabin in the mountains because his apartment in the city was too small for all of us. Earlier, I had drawn building plans, and had them approved for an addition to the cabin to make it more livable. This was my first experience to design and draw plans, and I used a set of plans from a contractor as a model to know how to go about it. My husband continued to live and work during the week in the city. Since we were a one-car family, I didn't have a car to return to Los Angeles to continue my training with the concert pianist.

Since 1970, I had enjoyed reading diaries and biographies that I borrowed from the Honolulu Public Library, to learn to read with more comprehension, and to learn more about how people think, feel, talk and write. I had begun in the children's section of the library to overcome my difficulties with reading comprehension, and a year later I began with a Philosophy course at a Community College.

Gift Through the Air

More recently, I had heard about Ann Morrow Lindbergh's diaries. Very soon after moving to the mountains with my son and daughter, one day, a thought came to me to go to the library, and check out her diaries.

The first book I chose was *Bring Me a Unicorn*.[1] Ann was very expressive in describing her thoughts and feelings, and the diary of her courtship with Charles Lindbergh was enchanting. He courted her, by taking her on some of his airplane trips, and she described the farmlands they were flying over. For about a month, I was flying with them in my imagination.

A month later in August of 1983, my son and daughter needed a school physical exam, and I made an appointment with the local doctor. At our visit, I asked the doctor whether he had a patient who commuted to Los Angeles every week so I could go back to study with the concert pianist again. He said he did and gave me the name and phone number. I called that person, and he said he didn't drive to Los Angeles anymore. He then took my breath away when he said, "I have a friend that does, only you must be willing to *fly*!"

Later that day, I called that man, and he said he flew once a week into the Santa Monica airport (about 120 miles). He could only give me 45 minutes notice so I always needed to be ready day or night with my bag packed. For six months I flew until my husband bought me a car. Again I was led in an unusual way to get what I needed. The entire time I was reading Ann's diaries, I never thought about getting an airplane ride to go to my piano lessons. Through her book, I felt I had been prepared so I would say yes to accepting such an unexpected idea of airplane rides. My teacher, Bernardo, was thrilled because he had some students who were not practicing enough. He said to me, "How POSH! Now I can tell my other students that I have a student that wants to study piano so much that she *flies* to study with me."

Became Ill

When I became ill in 1984, I wondered why, even after having been such a late bloomer that God had led me to the opportunity to study with a master teacher in Los Angeles. I had traveled a great distance from Honolulu to study with a concert pianist, and now my good health and maybe even my life was being taken away?

In 1983, I had happily married, each of us bringing our teenagers to the marriage. My husband's business required frequent national and international travel on which I accompanied him. Soon the typical problems of juggling the responsibilities of wife, mother, and career preparations became very stressful. Added to those stresses and adjustments, differing communication skills unknowingly can affect everyone's ability to understand, resolve or harmonize each other's differences. Also, at that time I was preparing and having my first auditions with conductors to perform with a symphony orchestra at the age of 39. By 1984, these problems together with my own past memories became too stressful for me. *Love by itself was not enough to solve the complicated problems of double binds (mental/emotional traps).*

In July 1984 at the age of 40, just after returning from a science meeting in Europe, I was struck by a rare, rapidly-progressing mixed connective-tissue disease. I quickly became crippled with arthritis pain and was unable to walk, drive or write.

During the time I was ill, I had almost daily nightmares of rejection, feared talking on the telephone, and leaving my home. I became agoraphobic. It appeared that I was dying because I was deteriorating very rapidly. The doctors said there was no cure or medication I could take for the pain, as I was allergic to anti-inflammatory drugs. My physical and emotional pain was so acute that I wanted to eventually just die, and wished to die in peace. I desperately wanted to escape the pain of this life. As I mentally detached from everyone, I prepared myself in a number of ways, and began to feel some relief, gaining a greater clarity of mind.

My physical, mental, and emotional pain were so great that I was unable to sleep for more than minutes at a time. The pain, anguish and fear of what was happening would awaken me. I had always eaten a well-balanced diet, and exercised regularly, so food and exercise, based on the information I had at that time, were no additional source of treatment.

The rheumatologist told me there was no foreseeable cure, and I would possibly be in a wheel-chair in another month at the rate I was deteriorating. I didn't know how remission would be possible, and I did not want to heal anyway. I was without faith, hope or belief in my ever healing, or by then even a will to live. However, I did have faith that I was safe to die naturally. I just wanted to die in peace, and go to God. There seemed to be too many problems and no solutions. I still had not found the answers to my question of how to let go of fear and pain from memories. I wondered whether my unresolved fear, pain, and guilt in addition to my other stresses were contributing to my illness.

When facing death, I thought I would be leaving all my pain behind. I was escaping—I could no longer be hurt. I found some relief and safety in that thought. Because of that seeming safety and comfort, I was now able to think more clearly.

With some peace, my thoughts began to search for cause and effect. The contradiction of the wonderful synchronistic spiritual events in my life with the many painful experiences didn't seem to make sense. As for feeling "punishment," I had mostly been punishing myself with old conflicts, and had allowed others to punish me. That evening, just before falling asleep, I asked, "What is missing from the minds of people who don't do what is best for themselves and others?" In the middle of the night, I was awakened with a voice that said, "It's very simple—I'm always safe not hurting myself or others."

I realized that this message had been hidden, and confused, and that I needed to add, "when healthy for me," at the end of each of the messages of my method for a number of reasons. Many people have not asked themselves, "What is healthy and wise?" before making a choice. Also, "when healthy for me," addresses a paradox with hurt and safety—there are times when saying no to oneself or someone else may hurt, but is a wise healthy choice.

Then I created the method originally intended
just to give calm and peace that
unexpectedly cured me!

Gift of Peace and Inner Healing

In late February 1985, I put together a method, which I hoped would allow me to at least die in peace. Every day, every 2 hours, I used this new relaxation method. Throughout the day, when not doing my method, I would continuously replace painful thoughts with the new thoughts of my method.

Ten (10) days later, all the fear and pain from my past memories associated with particular people were gone! For me this was miraculous. Having suffered since I was a child, like many people I had accumulated even more fear and pain as I grew older. I still had the painful physical symptoms of the disease and continued to do the relaxation exercise every two hours each day.

Now feeling a high degree of emotional and spiritual peace, I waited in peace to die. After another two weeks of doing my relaxation exercise, all the physical pain left my body at once. I was astonished! I was more impressed by my emotional healing than my physical, because I had suffered since childhood. Also, for many years, I had worked through therapy to let go the pain of the past without results.

Immediately, I began to play piano eight hours a day again (too much, too soon) and relapsed. I pulled myself back, to work about four hours a day, continuing the relaxation exercise. The physical pain left again. Finally, I was able to listen and hear myself to choose a healthy balance in amount of food and my activity each day (saying no to under or over-doing), and remained in remission, gradually increasing my work hours.

After thinking about this, I realized *how my healing method worked to resolve and defuse many conflicts—(*initially, at least the intellectual aspects of many conflicts). Unexpectedly, this led me to a path of ever increasing light, which gave me the gift of *how to live in greater peace.*

After healing in 1985, I was asked to describe and demonstrate my method for letting go of fear, pain and stress to aid healing so quickly and effectively. I began presenting the method to some people who were suffering, and this led to being a Pain & Stress Consultant in several medical treatment centers in the Los Angeles area for many years.

My method is explained in Ch. 17: Path of Discovery (p. 201).

Later, while writing a paper describing this method, I analyzed why the particular details of the method seemed so dramatically effective and to work so rapidly in my healing process. However, I realized that other people are in different stages of understanding, and so I added additional messages, designed worksheets with additional procedures and guidance, and recorded two Peace and Inner Healing CDs; one for children and young people (ages 10 and up), and one for adults. These are to assist others with different backgrounds to more easily apply this method to achieve similar healing results. These tools, found in the Appendix, may aid you in using your logical reasoning powers *for* you instead of *against* yourself. My web site is www.apathtolight.com.

Another Aspect And Benefit

The peaceful repeated mental thought-patterns and attitudes of the messages of this method along with good will toward myself and others, created a high degree of inner peace which seemed to favorably affect my own immune system[2], thus aiding my physical healing.

Aside from this, there is another surprising aspect to the method in that, similarly, good-will prayerful thoughts and attitudes also seem to have a beneficial effect directly on others' attitudes.

Even though I had experienced some remarkable results with people changing in front of me, I had not fully realized how powerful it can be to just direct my prayerful thoughts towards those who are suffering. I had forgotten to do it regularly. Now, when confronted with sometimes angry or sad people in so much pain, I suddenly remembered, and began to focus on this thought in everyone's presence.

I was deeply moved by a person who was very angry and had recently attempted suicide. All of a sudden, I remembered that when I had lived in Hawaii, God had told me how to ease pain and create harmony—silently focus on the thought . . .

"I am always safe receiving and giving grace,
love and peace to you,"

. . . towards everyone, and especially those who are angry, irritable or sad. After actively focusing my thoughts of grace for the person mentioned above for a short period of time, the person's attitude changed dramatically—was more open and wanted to learn how to let go of pain in a healthy manner. At another time I did this for a couple I saw at a distance who were arguing in a restaurant, and they stopped. Another time I was buying a ticket at a concert. The ticket seller was very irritated, and after I quickly thought this thought, he changed and became kind.

Gift of Piano Lessons

Another example is when I was in training in my piano teacher's home to perform with an orchestra. My gifted master teacher, a world-renowned concert pianist, and composer, Bernardo Segall sometimes would get very frustrated with me (which is understandable) when I was not able to immediately perform a new piano technique. He would raise his voice with further explanations. I would tell him to not worry, because by the next week, I probably would be able to do it. I even told him that getting upset was not healthy for him. This did not change his frustration level much. As the tension in his voice raised, his wife, Beverly would gently open the door, and Jimmy Joe, their 6 ft. puppy dog (meaning he filled the 6 ft. couch in the piano room where he sprawled) came wandering into the room. You would think this would break the tension. No luck.

Finally, I remembered to focus silently on the thought, "I am safe receiving and giving grace, compassion, love and peace to you." Bernardo immediately began to calm down. We never had any more tension-filled episodes, because I would remember to silently think the above peaceful thought at the beginning signs of any excessive tension. He seemed to receive my non-audible prayerful communication.

Gift of Peace

Through another example, I was reminded again of just how powerful and protective this good-will thought is, by a very unexpected experience. This experience propelled me into a very serious confrontation with potential violence.

One afternoon a very upset mother who had several young children came to my door. She said her husband from whom she had been separated for quite some time, and in divorce proceedings, was very distraught. She said he was in her house with several of their young children and had a gun. Her other young child was in school. The mother had just obtained a restraining order, and came to ask me to deliver it for her, rather than a paid process server. She said because she knew of my healing method, and knew I was a person of peace, she thought that I would be able to deliver the restraining order without inflaming her husband's volatile (unstable, potentially explosive) state. I felt this was going to be a test of just how protective this healing method is for all of us. I quickly told the Mother to silently give her husband and children grace, love and peace while we were driving to her house, as well as during the time I was delivering the restraining order.

I drove to their home, and the mother arrived, but stood back near her car. I knocked on the door. Her husband opened the door looking very distraught. I explained that I needed to give him these papers to create safety for him and everyone. He took the papers, tore them, and threw them on the floor slamming the door. The mother said she was calling the sheriff for assistance, and we both left.

At that time, I didn't know that I would later be called to testify in court. Because of the husband's angry behavior, I didn't know whether he would retaliate against me or would my healing method protect us. A friend of mine who is a retired sheriff offered to drive behind me to make sure I would get to the courthouse safely. He also said he had called a friend of his, a former bodyguard to King Hussein, to also meet us there to protect us. I was in a state of wonder that in an unusual way my safety had been provided for again.

The day arrived, and after having only a brief time before I testified in court, I again explained to the mother that she could silently give her husband grace, love and peace to protect them all, which she said she would. The court proceeded and dealt with the matter and the problems became resolved. A different constructive path may be traveled earlier, when there is an opportunity to quickly learn and act with a nurturing method. This gives people the tools to discuss differences more harmoniously—deal with uncomfortable thoughts, feelings, and behavior to arrive at healthy comfort, and let go of unnecessary fear, pain and guilt in a healthy manner.

Gift of Good-Will

You can *silently* give good-will anywhere—in a grocery store when you see a parent upset with a child or any upset person, while driving to prevent road-rage, on the job, at a hospital visit, a sporting event, etc.

In the beginning, you may not feel or be entirely sincere about what you are repeating(because your fear, pain, and guilt may be in the way).

As you focus on any of the messages of this method, it is important to be consciously aware of the meaning of the messages you are repeating. After some time focusing on these messages, you may experience a release of your depression, fear and pain, and greater sincerity can be felt. This requires focused attention to have a more immediate effect, which in time can be gained just by doing. This very concentrated repetition is like a child rehearsing for a spelling bee, or a person memorizing and knowing new lines for a play.—You benefit through concentration and focus, and gain these just by doing.

In my book, *A Path to Light*, I include some letters from people, which tell of their experiences of successfully using the healing method.

Their experiences and mine are a reminder of just how beneficial the prayerful thought "I'm always safe receiving and giving grace, compassion, love and peace to you when healthy for me," is in letting go of sadness, anger, and violence. I ask you to experiment to see for yourself the transforming power of this thought. People may transform and/or walk away peacefully. Focusing one's own thought pattern on a peaceful giving attitude toward another seems often to have an effect on other's attitude. This phenomenon appears to happen often enough to merit experimenting. Just how the transference is effected—the mechanism—is more speculative (subtle visual cues, pheromones, electromagnetism, etc.)—a separate subject for contemplation or research. Meanwhile, I think of it as a universal grace prayer, and it seems to travel long-distance.

There are many benefits in imagining sending your silent thoughts of grace, compassion, love and peace to others. You don't have to block yourself from enjoying life by continuing to either numb yourself from painful feelings, or continue with sadness, resentment or anger, which can *color* the rest of your other experiences.

Gift of Awakening

When a neighbor's son had been in a car accident and was in the hospital in a coma, I had a very unusual experience. After a number of weeks, I felt so sad for her that I offered to go to the hospital and see whether my prayerful thoughts could aid in bringing him out of the coma. One evening, while sitting with them in their hospital room, I focused on the thought of, "I'm giving you grace, love and peace, and you are safe to come back." After a half hour nothing had changed, and I was tired, so I said I would go home. I walked across the room and opened the door to leave when all of a sudden her son spoke, saying, "MaMa." He came out of his coma and started slowly speaking to his mother. The next day, I called Dr. Baron who at that time was at the University of Southern California School of Medicine. He offered to go and visit the young man in the County Hospital and read his chart. He said, the doctors had "written nothing remarkable in his chart." Who knows for sure.

If you have a loved one in a coma, you, along with your family and friends may want to experiment, individually as well as a group, giving your loved one grace, compassion, love and peace and letting them know they are safe to come back. Maybe they will respond.

Ideas that affected my healing process:

When I was ill and seemed to be dying, I thought that I would like to die naturally and in peace since I had known very little peace in living. Because of the few wonderful experiences I had had in life were associated with the spiritual dimension, I was ready to go to heaven. That was the only place where I thought I would feel and be safe. I began to think of myself as safe, and also approved of by God, because I *had* been given *some* wonderful opportunities, even though there only seemed to be a few. In my mind, I let the few wonderful experiences weigh more, and diminished the weight of the large amount of painful ones. Before this, I had thought and felt unworthy. I had hardly ever felt approval and acceptance. I did know that I had good intentions.

Although, I had made mistakes like everyone else, nevertheless I had been given a number of amazing spiritual experiences. Because of this, I finally realized that we are *valuable* just because we have the *gift of life*, even though I had not been treated this way by everyone. Many had learned confusing beliefs. I made up my mind that I would no longer rely on people who are punishing and destructive. They were not a healthy model. I am relying on God, myself, and kind people.

Spontaneously, I began to think about the concept of grace, which means forgiveness, mercy, compassion, and unmerited love. I saw this as innately universal (for all people), and that this concept did not include punishment. Finally, using a new perspective in logic, I saw that since God is Grace, I could stop the punishment by being in Grace in my thoughts and actions. In the state of Grace, I am not punishing myself or others. Without realizing it at the time, I had untangled what had been a confusing knot for me. For me, compassion and forgiveness for others were not the problems. It was for myself, and how to stop the repetitive flashbacks of fear and pain from memories. Then how to accomplish this (as far as stopping the unnecessary repetitive fear, pain, and guilt from memories) was the challenge.

When I fell asleep that night I asked God the question: "What is missing from the minds of people who do not do what is best for themselves?" I fell asleep and in the middle of the night with a voice in my thoughts that said,

"It's very simple. I am always safe not hurting myself, you or others."

After reflecting, I realized that this *is* the state of grace and compassion. Focusing on this message begins the release from punishment (announcing a new change—in safety). This message seems to have been missing, or confused and hidden from many people's minds. The questions are why and how? Some detailed answers are addressed in my book, *A Path to Light*. Also, as I mentioned earlier, I added, "when healthy for me."

Silently focusing on, *"I'm always safe receiving and giving grace, love and peace to myself and others,"* furthered my release from punishment. The fact that some messages are missing or hidden and confused explains why many people, even when they knew what was good for them, didn't choose that path, or when on it for a while, they quit. The following is an example:

Maintain Healthy Habits?

One of the problems you may have experienced is how to maintain new healthy habits. For example: Research studies demonstrate that relaxation and exercise programs benefit general health and the immune system (and thereby resistance to disease) in young and old.[3, 4, 5]

However, a *significant observation* in one such study was made in a later follow-up on a group of subjects who had definitely benefited from such a program [i.e., had shown improved measures of immune function, and had spontaneously reported being much more aware and enjoyed the program]. Researchers noted that later, surprisingly, only a quarter of them "reported setting aside regular periods of time for relaxation such as they had during the training period."[6]

EVEN THOUGH IT'S GOOD FOR YOU

The problem in *any new healthy program* seems to be how to continue doing it, *even though it's good for you!*

> "Come, there's no use in crying like that!" said Alice to herself, rather sharply, "I advise you to leave off this minute!" She generally *gave herself very good advice* (though she *very seldom followed it*), and sometimes she scolded herself so severely as to bring tears into her eyes . . . [7]

With this healing method, you can safely add new thought processes so you may resolve conflicts, solve some double binds (mental/emotional traps), more easily let go of fear and pain, and make many more wise enjoyable choices. You then may control and transform your thoughts, feelings and behavior—your responses to stress in the present—in a more effective and harmonious manner. Then you can focus on the thought, "I receive and give myself healthy advice, and I folllow it," and may get the results. This allows you to enjoy being self-motivated to do what is healthy for you (follow healthy advice), so then you want to and *do continue.*

Relaxation Exercise

In my relaxation exercise, I silently repeated a few key statements, which I hoped would allow me to die in peace, but unexpectedly I healed. The *abbreviated* statements follow:

1. I am always safe knowing and living truth when healthy for me.
2. I am always safe not hurting myself, you and others when healthy for me.
3. I am always safe letting go fear, pain, guilt and punishment with myself, mother, father, and _____ (siblings, people, animals, etc.) when healthy for me.
4. I am always safe receiving and giving grace, compassion, love and peace to myself, mother, father, _____ (siblings, animals, and all people) when healthy for me.
5. I am always safe and healed when healthy for me.

Intuitively, I also focused on a pulse throughout my body (one area at a time). It was to experiment as if I had a telephone hookup to all parts of my body and could ring them up at will. I silently repeated, "I'm always safe feeling my pulse in and around _____." I was imagining "sending healing twinkle star cells" to each part of my body, and "disappearing the cells causing the pain, stiffness and swelling." I did this without any faith, belief or hope that this would work. I did have faith that I was safe to die naturally which gave me some peace of mind.

My bio-feedback technique (feeling a pulse) has the additional advantage of distracting your mind from destructive thoughts and emotions so you may achieve homeostasis (balance).

Researchers state that cells in our body are known to respond to mechanical stimuli (such as alternating pressure from the pulse) and differentiate accordingly to alter their metabolic behavior. For example, new cartilage cells appearing in certain lesions of the arterial wall, primarily as a result of the pulsation effect regenerate through the intermittent pressure.[8]

It is well known that cartilage cells in our joints respond to load bearing pressures such as walking, and that they atrophy during disuse.

A Chinese physician trained both in Chinese and Western medicine once told me he thought focusing on a pulse in my healing method may be similar to what acupuncture and acupressure have been doing.

It is easiest to feel your pulse in your hands and fingers. Sit or lie down in a comfortable position and close your eyes. With the palms of your hands facing up—(using your mind), feel a pulse in your hands and fingers, and repeat silently: "I'm always safe feeling my pulse in my hands and fingers.

When I was ill, I was not in a relaxed state because of so much physical and emotional pain. Because of having an allergic reaction to anti-inflammatory drugs which affected my breathing, I was unable to take any for my pain. I simply had an attitude of experimentation and wanted to die without emotional pain if at all possible.

Every two hours I would do the half-hour relaxation exercise focusing on the thoughts of my healing method, including relaxing my muscles, feeling a pulse, and sending healing cells. I did this even though I couldn't actually feel the meaning of my thoughts or totally relax. When not doing the exercise, I would continue to focus on these thoughts throughout the day by persistent repetition.

Also, *when falling asleep*, I would repeat each of the *above 5 messages 4 times*. Sometimes I got very tired of doing this. Then I would take short breaks, and remind myself that I had been spending a lot of time and energy thinking painful thoughts, so I might as well use the same time and energy thinking the new harmonious thoughts. Day after day I continued this pattern, because it increasingly seemed to make sense. By focusing on new constructive thoughts, I was interrupting the pattern of painful thoughts, which then led me to *feel new constructive emotions.*

Even when I had a simple sore throat, I focused on, "I'm safe feeling my pulse in and around my cheeks, throat and jaw." (also, I just focused on my throat.) Then, I silently thought "I'm safe sending healing twinkle star cells in and around my cheeks, throat, and jaw." I did this for 10-15 min, and my throat irritation disappeared."

Silent Thoughts

Later, when I wrote my first paper on the healing method, in addition to sharing the method, wrote how the idea of an actively directed prayer process of silent thoughts may also aid in stopping violence.

Some reasons why many have held on to depression, fear and pain, as well as how the expression of anger in the form of *healthy assertiveness,* rather than irritability or rage may aid your immune system are explained in Chapter 17: Path of Discovery.

In 1987, when I was in church, the minister told about ministers recently being imprisoned in South Africa. He gave their addresses, and asked for prayers and letters to be sent to them. I mailed them my paper on healing.

Because of experiencing the dramatic results of using the healing method—creating harmony for others when directing one's prayerful thoughts towards them—I also thought of the people of South Africa that had suffered so much violence. I was moved to reach them through my paper.

[1]   Lindbergh, Ann Morrow, *Bring Me A Unicorn,* (1922-1928), (New York, Harcourt Brace Jovanovich, Inc., 1971).

[2]   Goleman, Daniel, "Doctors Find Comfort Is a Potent Medicine," *Science,* November 26, 1991.

[3]   Solomon, George, MD; Fiatarone, Maria; Benton, Donna; Morley, John; Bloom, Eda; Makinodan, Takashi; "Psychoimmunologic and Endorphin Function in the Aged," *Annals of the New York Academy of Sciences*, March 29, 1988, Vol. 521.

[4]   Fiatarone, Maria; Morley, John; Bloom, Eda; Benton, Donna; Solomon, George; Makinodan, Takashi; "The Effect of Exercise on Natural Killer Cell Activity in Young and Old Subjects," *Journal of Gerontology: MEDICAL SCIENCES*, 1989, Vol. 44, No. 2, M37-45.

[5]   Kiecolt-Glaser, Janice; Glaser, Ronald; et al; "Psychosocial Enhancement of Immunocompetence in a Geriatric Population," 1985, *Health Psychology*. 4: 24-41.

[6]   *Ibid.*, p. 39.

[7]   Carroll, Lewis, *Alice's Adventures in Wonderland*, Compiled & Arranged by Cooper Edens, (New York, Bantam Books, 1989, p 21).

[8]   Rodbard, Simon, "Negative Feedback Mechanisms in the Architecture and Function of the Connective and Cardiovascular Tissues," Perspectives Biology and Medicine, 1969-1970, 13:507-527.

5. PROMOTING HEALING AND PEACE

Opening Blossoms

Opening blossoms turn to light
Receiving warmth—glow of Life
Giving radiance, embracing others
Renewing raindrops, shimmering showers

Reaching others, sharing truth
Releasing binds blinding youth
Now letting go, let your face show,
Let poison go, let your life flow

Bejewelling blossoms, inspiring more
Heartening hearts, impelling lore
Knowing the gift, giving to you
Reaching in time, saving earth too

Dispelling darkness leads to Life
Choosing, follow shining Light
Loving within—letting go strife
Nurturing blossoms giving Life

(Written 1976)

IN 1987, ANOTHER EXCITING adventure began when, through my thoughts, I was told to also mail my paper to Bishop Tutu of South Africa to aid in creating peace. A few weeks later in February '87, I was told to take my paper to the Archbishop of Canterbury in order to help Terry Waite, an emissary for the Church of England. He, himself had just been taken hostage in troubled Lebanon while negotiating on behalf of a number of hostages taken a few months previously. Since I had no connections with the Church of England, I wondered how I would accomplish this. Just the summer before, my husband and I had been in Canterbury on a 2-day visit to the University of Kent. (At that time I had no idea I would soon become involved with hostage-release and the Archbishop of Canterbury.)

One day we had had lunch at a charming restaurant near the ancient Canterbury Cathedral. It was at this historic "Mayflower Inn" (in 1620 the pilgrim ship 'Mayflower' was named for it) where the many Puritans in the town of Canterbury had met to discuss their brethren temporarily exiled in Holland for religious freedom, and later to plan their Pilgrim emigration to America. [This later turned out to be another hidden connection to my future soul mate!]

We were already preparing to go to England in a few weeks (the end of February). My husband and I traveled there about three times a year for scientific meetings and to visit his mother. When in England, I usually would go to a local church, where I also had been given permission to use their piano to maintain my piano skill. I thought very *simply* that I would just ask the Vicar at the church for the Archbishop of Canterbury's address at Canterbury Cathedral. Then I could mail him my paper on aiding in the release of Terry Waite.

In London, at the end of February, when I awakened on Sunday morning, there was a wild wind and rainstorm. There was no way I could venture out to church and get the address. I then thought to call a friend nearby in London, who was a representative of B'nai B'rith. On our last trip to London she had told me that the year before, through the Council of Christians and Jews, B'nai B'rith had organized and given a music festival in Canterbury Cathedral. Because of this, I thought that she might know the Archbishop's address. I called my friend, and she told me that the Archbishop lived in Lambeth Palace in London, *not* in Canterbury and gave me his address.

As I was writing down the address, my friend gave me very startling news: She said that she had been invited along with many other members of B'nai B'rith to Lambeth Palace that very next Wednesday evening. It was the first time in the 800-year history of Lambeth Palace (the residence of the head of the Church of England} that any Jewish people had been invited there. The Archbishop's wife was giving a piano recital in aid of a B'nai B'rith Music Festival.

Unexpectedly, my friend said, "Come with me, and give your paper in person!" I began to shake with excitement as an adventure was unfolding in a most unimagined way. I never dreamed this could happen. Because of the excitement, I was unable to sleep for three days. This is another example of how I have a few simple hints, and then am led to unexpected, extraordinary events.

A month earlier on February 3, 1987, I had sent a copy of my paper on healing and how to end violence to Bishop Tutu of South Africa. I had received a postcard from his office that he was away traveling, and that they would have him read my paper when he returned. At the time I mailed my paper to Bishop Tutu, I had no idea that I would be taking my paper to the Archbishop in London, just a month later.

On March 2, 1987, the day before we were to go to Lambeth Palace, I read in the newspaper that Bishop Tutu was giving a lecture in London the day we would be returning to Los Angeles. I prepared a second copy of my paper to take with me to the Palace. That evening, March 3, 1987, my friend drove us into the historic Lambeth Palace, past massive stone walls, shadowy gray in the light of ancient-looking lanterns. I felt we were living an old fashioned fairy-tale. We walked up stairs and through long carpeted hallways hung with many oil paintings.

After the Archbishop's wife played her beautiful piano recital, my friend introduced me to some of her group. As we all moved down the long hallway toward the reception, one of the men in her group jokingly remarked to me that it had taken them 800 years to get in here—how did I get in here overnight? I replied, "It's an enchanting mystery to me, too!"

At the reception, my friend introduced me to the Archbishop's wife, remarking that I had just come from America to give the Archbishop a paper to help gain freedom for Terry Waite. She thanked me and said she would give it to her husband. I told her that I had also brought an extra copy for Bishop Tutu, and asked if she knew how to reach him? She replied that he was coming for lunch that very Sunday, and she would give it to him. I received several letters from the Archbishop of Canterbury's office thanking me for my paper and concern. It took another four years and a lot of money to free Terry Waite and the other hostages, but they did return safely. (Later, Lambeth Palace turned out to be another connection to my future soul mate.)

Why was I so moved to action in this peace-emissary Terry Waite/peacemaker Bishop Tutu/Lambeth Palace experience? I recall my mother telling me that when I was 6 years old, in post-war Japan, watching missionaries in the field helping people, I had said "That's what I want to be when I grow up!" Little did I know that my training would be unusual—getting a disease, healing, presenting my healing method to others, and writing books on healing.

Divine Timing

Clouds flowing through cradle of Life, we enter through a prayer
Unmeasured time being here, underneath all, people who care
Reflections, lost souls in space, quietly having not left their place
Don't let this be you, before too late, hearts opening heaven's gate

Reaching suffering souls in time, glorious path, only breath away
Release your cares, pain of claims, knowing it's not too late
Fantasy walk, sometimes fair, never in emptiness can compare
Life fully given, love to all, compassion, joyous cross to bear

Time, courier of pain can be, for those locked in despair
Time to go on, heart overflowing, being no more to clear
Eternally rejoicing, path ending pain, time you may thought lost
Growing through time, spiritual gain, passing time only the cost

Blessings always where we are, beyond, anytime can be found
Guided silently by Love, Sun, Moon, rapturous merry-go-round
Divine timing, grace—simply one with all, time floating, play of its own
Miracle, glowing Spiritual Light, surrounding, protecting from the throne

(Written 1993)

After returning from London in March, I began a new venture. In April 1987, psychiatrist, David Baron, D.O., became a consultant on my clinical work. Dr. Baron is the former Deputy Director of the National Institute of Mental Health, in Bethesda, MD, and his other positions are mentioned in the Acknowledgements. Now he is Professor and Vice-Chair, Dept. of Psychiatry Keck School of Medicine, and Psychiatrist-in-Chief, Keck Medical Center at USC, Los Angeles.

That April 1987, I began consulting in a health-care clinic in the Los Angeles area, and walked people through my method so they could walk out of darkness into the light. These people were of different racial, philosophical and religious backgrounds. They were suffering with various problems—from stress in their jobs and lives, people with arthritis, cancer, abuse, addictions, and some with AIDS.

The next year in April 1988, I began presenting to people having cancer and AIDS in another medical treatment center in the Los Angeles area. Also, during that time I went on another very unexpected adventure that led me to Lourdes, France.

6. HEALING WATERS

HOW I WAS LED to Lourdes is another unexpected mystical spiritual story. On one of my trips to London in 1987, a scientist, who knew about my healing work, said I might be interested in Lourdes, France. The next day I went to downtown London where there is a famous row of old bookstores and found the book *The Mystery of Lourdes*.[8] I read that there had not been very many healings in comparison to all the people who traveled there, and also that there were children and adults who healed who seemed to have no faith or belief. The mystery of my Fleur-de-lis lily pin came back to me.

First Trip to Lourdes Spring, France

A few months later in December, while my husband was in a science meeting in Bordeaux, I went to Lourdes. Around 5:30 AM I boarded a train. It was a very icy cold damp foggy winter morning, with very heavy cloud cover. A few miles before the train was to pull in to Lourdes, I began to pray. I asked God to please let the sun shine through, because I wanted to sit outside near the spring, and pray for the people who were so ill and maybe dying. When I got off the train I couldn't believe my eyes. The clouds began to part from the middle in an ever-increasing circle. I had never noticed clouds doing this before. Usually they move from one side to another.

After disembarking the train, I walked in an expanding circle of warm sunlight into the courtyard. There were only about 10 people in the huge courtyard because of the winter cold. I went and sat by the spring to pray. The grotto was in such a beautiful setting with the Pyrenees Mountains in the background. As I was sitting there, I was thinking about the book on Lourdes I had bought in London. In the book it was stated that although some people with faith had healed, there were children and adults without faith or belief who also had healed.

> Emotional shock . . . suggestion . . . psychic factors these are among the most popular of the tentative 'solutions.' People often speak of the abnormal emotionalism and suggestibility of the patients. That such a condition can bring about improvement or sudden cures of neurotics has been observed in various hospitals as well as at places of pilgrimage.
> But in many cures this element has been lacking: in the cures of the incredulous, of unbelievers, and of young children; in cures that have occurred at home, or on the return journey after all hope was given up; in cures elsewhere than at the baths or at the procession in Lourdes; and in cures that have occurred after two or more pilgrimages.[9]

While I was sitting there, hearing the spring, and praying for others, I began to think that maybe there might be something in the water along with the spiritual energy contributing to the healings—a spiritual gift in the water itself! What could it be?

Yamabuki-no-Omizu Spring, Japan

After we flew back to California, a few months later, mysteriously a book came to me from a stranger. It was called *Miracle Cure: Organic Germanium* by Kazuhiko Asai, Ph.D, on research in Japan. Dr. Asai had a doctorate in technology from the University of Kyoto. In this book were pictures of the spring in Lourdes, France, and also a rural spring, Yamabuki-no-Omizu (Mountain Rose Spring) in Japan on the northern tip of the Island of Honshu; both springs known for healings.

Because Dr. Asai was working on coal research after WWII, he was studying contaminants in coal for the steelmaking industry. In 1948 when germanium transistors were invented, the traces of germanium in coal became important as perhaps a source for transistors

In studying the microscopic distribution of germanium in coal, he deduced that it must have been a natural and useful part of the original plants that had become coal. Therefore, he tested many present-day plants such as bamboo, tea leaves, oak leaves, chlorella, etc. He found that plants containing large quantities of germanium were those also valued as ancient Chinese medicinal herbs. This led him to measure the germanium content in plants known for their beneficial effects in the treatment of malignant tumors.

Dr. Asai wrote that he thought that the spiritual development of a person also played a role in the success of a medicine or treatment. He also analyzed some water from Lourdes, and found it contained a high amount of germanium. (Was this the healing 'something in the water' I had wondered about at Lourdes just a few months before?) His curiosity then led him to analyze water from various curative springs in Japan. The Yamabuki-no-Omizu captured his attention, and upon analysis of its waters, he found it to have even higher concentrations of germanium than at Lourdes.

After 10 years of many approaches, in 1967, his research staff was able to synthesize a suitable water-soluble organic compound of germanium technically termed carboxy ethyl sesquioxide of germanium. Dr. Asai tested this on himself. At 60, he had a deteriorating physical condition diagnosed as polyrheumatism complicated by arthritis. He healed quickly, and then went on to give it to others who also healed. Dr. Asai also emphasizes the importance of diet, along with the use of germanium sesquioxide.

Since soon I was going to Japan in September 1988, with my husband who had a meeting in Tokyo, I immediately thought that I would like to visit Dr. Asai's Germanium Research Institute also in Tokyo.

Contact in Japan

A few days later, early in the morning, I received a telephone call from a man I had known for about a year and a half, who also worked at the same treatment center in Los Angeles. He had written a book on many of the cancer treatments in the world, and wanted to know when I was leaving for Japan. After giving him my schedule, I told him about Dr. Asai's book. Then I asked him what he knew about germanium—he had only briefly mentioned it in two sentences in his own book. He was blasé, and said it had not passed the FDA approval in Japan. I said that I plan to go and visit Dr. Asai's Clinic while in Tokyo. He didn't respond to that, and we hung up.

Early the next morning, he called me again, and asked me whether I was *really intent* on going to Dr. Asai's Germanium Clinic in Tokyo. I said that I was, and then he told me a most surprising story. He said that when Dr. Asai was alive, they were close friends. He advised me to write to the manager of the Asai Clinic, mention his name, and the manager would then take me into the clinic and show me everything.

This is another example of the wonderful synchronicity in the spiritual dimension. Dr. Asai's book came to me from someone I didn't know. The colleague I had known for over a year unexpectedly had been a close friend of Dr. Asai.

Very excited, I wondered how we could bring that particular purified high dose of medical non-lead germanium compound from Dr. Asai's lab to the U.S. It was reported to be non-toxic. Because of its reported beneficial effects on the immune system, we could set up a protocol in this country to assess its results on AIDS and cancer patients in conjunction with my healing method. Dr. Asai had mentioned in his book that he thought that the healing power of a medicine was also strongly affected by people's attitudes. I was told that germanium was presently available only in health food stores as a food supplement in low doses, and to check because some may be contaminated with lead.

Immediately I called Dr. David Baron, who at that time was the Deputy Director of the National Institute of Mental Health and a consultant on my research project. I asked whether he could assist me to write a protocol to test results of Dr. Asai's germanium along with my healing method here in the U.S. He gave me some ideas, and I mailed my letter to the manager at Dr. Asai's Research Institute. I received a reply from the manager in Japan writing that he didn't know how we could cooperate; however, he *would* meet with me at my hotel when I was in Tokyo.

Trip to Japan

After arriving in Tokyo, the manager came to my hotel to meet with me. Unexpectedly, he brought me research papers[10] to bring back to the U.S. to give to Dr. Baron. He had checked through a contact in Washington D.C. to see whether Dr. Baron was who I said he was. He was being cautious because some people had tried to take their method.

Also, I was given the names of some people in the National Cancer Institute (NCI) who were also doing research with Germanium. I called Dr. Baron from Japan to give him the contacts.

After returning to Los Angeles, I called Dr. Baron. He said he had gone right away to see the people in the National Cancer Institute (NCI) whom I had told him about in my call from Japan. Dr. Baron said they were going to quit working on their project with germanium because they didn't know how it worked. We then found we couldn't get permission to bring the Asai germanium to the United States for further research. We were extremely disappointed as all the doors seemed closed. [A decade later they seemed to be opening after all].

Concert

From September 1988 until April 1989, I also had the responsibility of organizing and performing as solo pianist with the Los Angeles Doctors' Symphony Orchestra and 5 professional choirs for a charity fund-raising concert for the first time as well.

Then I turned my focus, and put my energies into organizing the ecumenical concert for which I had passed an audition in the month before, and continued my consulting for people.

I still felt distraught that there was now no way to experiment with the Asai Germanium compound.

During my concert preparations, a research paper was given to me titled "HIV Seroprevalence in Newborns in New York State."[11] I was shaken by the statistics of *innocent babies* born with HIV in one city, together with many people I was consulting for in late stages of cancer, scleroderma and AIDS.

I made the following note on the margin of the research paper: "This and my consulting for people with chronic diseases moves me to go back to Lourdes, and bring back the water to give to the people, and get research results."

Since some researchers had reported the water at Lourdes contained possibly significant amounts of Germanium (although less than the dosage used by Dr. Asai.), I felt compelled and started planning to go back to Lourdes myself. I wanted to take some people there, and monitor their results in combination with my healing method, as well as bring back the water for others. With two local research laboratories, I set up to do tests and follow-up data on the effects of the germanium water from Lourdes. These were to be done for some of the people, with whom I had been consulting.

Second Trip to Lourdes

Just before the concert, the people had become too ill to risk their traveling, so then after the concert, I asked my son to go with me to bring back the water. In May, after a short trip to Florida to see my relatives, my son and I took 120 empty liter bottles in 6 suitcases to Lourdes. Our trip took us about 5 days to go and return. At the spring, there were thousands and thousands of children and adults in wheel chairs and on stretchers. This was another unexpected confrontation with massive suffering for which I was not prepared.

Many years later, I read a biography of Karen Horney, psychiatrist, in which the author shared the touching line given by a person in therapy.

"If it were not for reality, I would be perfectly all right.[12]

This was how I sometimes felt during the several months leading up to, and after returning from Lourdes. Like many of you, I experienced deep feelings responding to the great suffering of others that I saw, for which there are no adequate words.

After we returned, I immediately gave two weeks supply of the water to each person, and mailed bottles to two others. By the time I returned, one person had become too sick to drink the water and died in June. Some others had also become more severely ill and died soon after. Back to catch up with my other consulting, reports and correspondence, I was physically and emotionally depleted. I could do no more.

Burnout

I wasn't aware that I was not processing fast enough, and letting go of the overwhelming amount of pain of others that I was seeing and feeling. Because of taking on so much responsibility, budgeting my time became a problem and sometimes I didn't have the time to spend alone doing my own method on myself to release the pain of others. I mistakenly thought I was letting go of enough of their pain while I was leading them through the exercise of letting go. In addition to my other responsibilities,

I was involved in rehearsing with an orchestra every week for eleven weeks, as well as handling all the planning between orchestra and choirs, publicity, scheduling rehearsal halls and designing the program, etc. Also during that time, in order to put on a fund-raising concert, a law firm was setting up a non-profit foundation for me pro bono. All that complicated paperwork had to be handled quickly.

After the concert was finished on April 16, 1989, I didn't realize that I was completely exhausted, and didn't know what serious burnout felt like, much less how to prevent it.

In his book *Opening Up*,[13] James W. Pennebaker, Ph.D. shares the following about burnout:

> Burnout, in many respects, is a problem of inhibition. One of the dangers of repeatedly being confronted by other people's traumas is that there is little opportunity to talk about them. The symptoms of burnout are not limited to individuals in the helping professions. They can occur among friends of traumatized individuals.

Handling one emergency after another with an overloaded schedule, I was not aware of burnout. My mind was so preoccupied with so much to do. At that time, there also was no way for others around me or myself, to know or prevent the trap of burnout.

Symptoms of Burnout

In looking back at that period of time, I can see there may have been some clues. In meetings at the law firm, I would get dizzy from the language and the added paper work.

One day when I had to go downtown to City Hall to file for the permit for the concert, I was about to cross the street when a homeless person asked me for money. I gave him some money, and then began crying as I continued across the street. I felt extremely sad and frustrated at knowing what I know that might assist him to get out of the state of homelessness—frustrated that I didn't have a way to share my healing method with him. In the past I had offered to volunteer for two different organizations that aided the homeless in Los Angeles, to present my method, but procedures were too complicated. I had been approached by homeless people in the past, living in Santa Monica, and even though I felt sad for them, I had never begun crying.

Later on, months after the concert, my burnout and return, I typed some of the messages of the healing method on narrow slips of paper to hand out along with some money to homeless people that I met. In my public seminars, I also gave out these slips of paper so that others could do the same.

A week after the concert, my husband and I flew to Florida where he had a meeting, and we visited with my relatives. I had the feeling that I did not want to leave and return home to Los Angeles. I didn't realize that I wanted to run away from all the pressure and grief.

A week later, my son and I left for Lourdes, France, as scheduled, to collect the water for an experimental treatment for people with arthritis, scleroderma, cancer and AIDS.

Exhausted, around the end of May, I quit consulting, and went back East to be with my family and rest. I didn't want to return to Los Angeles.

The Way Back to Myself and Others

A month later while watching a movie, "The Dead Poet's Society," it made a sudden poignant turn reflecting deep suffering. When this happened, I began to sob uncontrollably. Suddenly I recognized that I was not just exhausted. I was also running away from all the pain and loss of those in late stages of disease with whom I had been working. I had not realized that I was not letting go of enough of my own pain, induced in sympathy with those that had suffered, had died, and may die, as well as their families. In the movie, suddenly, at last I saw what had happened to me. I had been able to hold together only until the concert was over, and had brought back the water from Lourdes delivering to all the people with illnesses. I had been handling one emergency after another, and emotionally collapsed like many people do after handling an emergency. No one around me, including myself, was familiar with this "occupational burnout" as it is called.

After watching the movie, I realized that in order for me to go back and again present my method to others, I needed to adjust my own point of view. I reminded myself that my healing method had *aided* people and their families to relieve their suffering and *improved their quality of life*—even those who later passed away. I returned to Los Angeles to consulting, remembering to keep a healthy balance, and have had no more problems with burnout. Very sadly, my marriage didn't survive, and we later divorced. Years later, I did meet and marry my soul mate, and we have been happily married for years.

In my book, *A Path to Light*, are included letters and some short studies selected from the hundreds of people, all of whom benefited from my preventive and healing method, many of whom I consulted for after my return.

Variables in Healing

There are many variables in the healing process. As to the germanium water from the Lourdes and Yamabuki-no-Omizu springs, there are many unanswered questions. What compounds of germanium are most effective? Just *how* does it work? Does the water have a higher level of germanium in different months, at different times of the month or day, and is it as concentrated now as it once was? Does it interact with other ingredients in the water that may be present in higher quantities at different times? What quantities of the water do people drink? Based on reports, not all people respond to Germanium, or the water at Lourdes, whether a person has faith or not. Of those that didn't respond, what was their diet and state of mind, etc.? How much does one's disposition, personal history, and position on different issues contribute? Are some young children more responsive to the water because they know less, and have greater inner peace?

In the Economist April 2000 issue,[14] it is reported that since 1862, only 66 of over 6,700 cures declared by pilgrims are considered "miraculous."

The following are two recent reports: In 1997, there is a research paper published called "Effect of pretreatment of germanium-132 on galactose cataracts."[15]

In February 2000 a research paper documents the remission of pulmonary spindle cell carcinoma after treatment with oral germanium sesquioxide in a patient who remains clinically and radiographically free of disease 42 months after starting her alternative therapy.[16] The dosage is also important.

Betty Kamen, Ph.D., in *Germanium: A New Approach to Immunity*,[17] refers to Dr. Asai's work, and gives some dietary suggestions of vegetables and herbs containing a high content of germanium.

In the spring of 1996, I stopped my long commute and consulting work in Los Angeles. I wanted to focus on completing my book on the preventive and healing method so that that *my healing method* could reach and be of benefit to *many more people.* Looking for references and research papers led me on further unexpected spiritual adventures.

---

8   Cranston, Ruth, *The Mystery of Lourdes*, (Great Britain, Garden City Press, Limited Letchworth, Hertfordshire, 1956).

9   *Ibid*, p. 214.

[10] Brutkiewicz, Randy R. and Suzuki, Fujio, "Biological Activities and Antitumor Mechanism of an Immunopotentiating Organogermanium Compound, Ge-132 (Review)." in vivo1: 189-204, Reprint requests to: R.R. Brutkiewicz, Department of Microbiology, Pharmaceutical Research and Development Division, Bristol-Myers Company, Wallingford, Connecticut 06492, 1987.

[11] Novick, Lloyd F., M.D.; Berns, Donald, PhD; Stricof, Rachael, MPH; Stevens, Roy PhD; Pass, Kenneth PhD; Wethers, Judith, MS.: "HIV Seroprevalence in Newborns in New York State, *JAMA*, March 24/31, 1989Vol 261, No. 12.

[12] Quinn, Susan, *A Mind Of Her Own, The Life of Karen Horney*, (New York, Summit Books, Inc., 1987), p. 393.

[13] Pennebaker, James, Ph.D., *Opening Up*, (William Morrow and Company, Inc. New York, N.Y., 1990), p. 127.

[14] Miracles under the microscope, *Economist*, Vol. 366, Issue 8167, p. 77, April 22, 2000.

[15] Unakar NJ, Tsui J, Johnson M, Effect of pretreatment of germanium-132 on Na(+)-K(+)-ATPase and galac tose cataracts, *Curr Eye Res*, 16(8):832-7, Aug 1997.

[16] Mainwaring MG, Poor C, Zander DS, Harman E., Complete remission of pulmonary spindle cell carcinoma after treatment with oral germanium sesquioxide., *Chest*, 117 (2): 591-3, Feb 2000.

[17] Kamen, Betty, Ph.D., *Germanium: A New Approach to Immunity*, (California, Nutrition Encounter, Inc., 1987) Eighth Printing 1997.

7. Spiritual Synchronicities

IN FEBRUARY 1993, TIME Magazine had an article written about the book, *The Science of Love*,[18] written by Anthony Walsh, Ph.D., professor of Sociology, Anthropology, and Criminal Justice at Boise State University, Idaho. When I read his book, I was moved by his understanding for the necessity for compassion. He wrote,

"*. . . for no culture has ever survived the loss of compassion.*[19]

Also, in referring to the memories of pain from the past he wrote,

"*Synaptic connections can also be pruned by disuse, just like a trail can disappear if no longer trodden . . .*"

Since the healing method I developed seems to allow this to happen, I thought that Dr. Walsh would understand what I had discovered. When I was writing a research grant proposal, I called Dr. Walsh to request copies of research papers I had read about in his book. He was very kind and recommended some good articles and books. When my manuscript was finished, I called and asked him to review it and make editing suggestions. He did, and was very encouraging and helpful.

In early June 1995, while doing research for my manuscript, I was in the Santa Monica Library looking for two books—one by R.D. Laing, M.D., psychiatrist, and one by Gregory Bateson, Ph.D., anthropologist, on their thoughts about the "double bind" (mental/emotional traps). Previously, I had read their books, and had forgotten to write down the sources. Both books were not on the shelf. Next to where R.D. Laing's book would have been was a book titled *Synchronicity*[21] by F. David Peat, Ph.D., physicist. This book captivated me. A physicist who writes about synchronicity. He might understand my discoveries and healing method.

While still standing in front of the book shelves, randomly I opened to page 199, and my eyes immediately fell on one particular sentence. Dr. Peat was referring to R.D. Laing, M.D., Gregory Bateson, Ph.D., and the "double bind." These were the two authors that I had specifically driven to the library to find their books, and their books were checked out. I knew then that I was in the middle of a *spiritual synchronistic* experience.

Then I was moved to randomly open to another page, and found myself in Chapter 8. There Dr. Peat was discussing his concerns on subjects that are directly related to my method. David Peat wrote that people have felt trapped by their pasts as well as the failings of society. Present conflicts have seemed inevitable and creative solutions have seemed out of reach. Among the many thoughtful questions he posed is the following:

> [Are we] limited by the static mental structures and social orders that have evolved over the past thousands and tens of thousands of years, or is consciousness fundamentally unlimited in its potential for change . . . ?[22]

Many people have been limited by their fears, pains, and mental/emotional traps created in language and belief systems for the purpose of trying to protect themselves from fear and pain.

David Peat adds:

> . . . but clearly [the question's] significance goes far beyond this particular field, and into the whole question of the future of the human race, and considering the threat of nuclear war, to the very survival of life on this planet.[23]

Because of his sincerity and background, I wrote to him, and did so in care of his publisher. My letter was returned because the publisher had changed address. Feeling ambivalent, I continued reading many books on physics, teaching myself some of the language of physics, and wrote the chapter Elliptical Light. I wanted to explain the healing method in the language of physics, and be able to talk with Dr. Peat about my discoveries.

Very soon afterward, I read *The Turbulent Mirror*,[24] by John Briggs, PhD psychologist and Dr. Peat. Then I was motivated to call John Briggs at a university in Connecticut to find an address for Dr. Peat. I left a message on John Briggs answering machine in early June 1995.

At the same time in early June, I was in a restaurant reading David Peat's book *The Philosopher's Stone*.[25] A man and his young son sat at a table next to mine. He asked me about the book, and told me about his interest and background in physics. We had an interesting discussion, and then went our separate ways.

Four months later in October, a series of events happened that *mirrored* the series of events that happened four months earlier with some variations! Missing my grown son and daughter, I went to eat in a restaurant where we sometimes went. There was the same man with his young son that I had met the previous June, only in a different restaurant! He invited me to have lunch with them. We discussed physics again. He asked me whether I had found a particular book on physics that he had mentioned the last time we met. The library didn't have a copy, so I had not read it. He told me where I could buy a copy. I shared that my manuscript had just reached my consultant, Dr. David Baron, psychiatrist, in Philadelphia two days before. Again we went our separate ways.

The following week when I was in Los Angeles I bought the book that he had mentioned. David Peat was mentioned in that book. When I returned that weekend to the mountains, one of my piano students said she had told a friend that I was a piano teacher. The lady wanted to give me some old piano books which she no longer needed. We met at the Post Office, and when I looked at the thin antique books, at first glance they appeared to be music books. After I opened them I could see they were not piano books at all! They were a large collection of books called *The Classic and the Beautiful from the Literature of Three Thousand Years*,[26] published in 1901 in Philadelphia, which is where I had just sent my manuscript.

Why had these books been given to me? Hoping to find the significance of these books, I opened the first volume and read on the first page, the last paragraph. "The Chinese, selections are given from Mih Teih also known as Mo Ti, who flourished about 400 B.C., and who advocated as a cure for all human ills, universal mutual love."

Again, I remembered the many stories of grace in the Bible; from the Old and New Testaments—in Genesis 37-48 Joseph and his Coat of Many Colors, through to the teachings of Jesus in Matthew, Mark, Luke and John.

For example, in Luke 6:27-28. Jesus said, "Love your enemies, do good to them that hate you. Bless them that curse you, and pray for them that despitefully use you."

Tears came to my eyes thinking about my healing method which aids in learning and living universal grace and compassion.

The day after receiving the books at the Post Office, I went for a walk in the forest to calm myself from all the excitement of my experience. Synchronistically, when I came home there was a message on my machine from John Briggs, Ph.D. in Connecticut, saying Dr. David Peat had just called him from London. David had given John his address and phone number for me to reach him. Four months had gone by since I left a message on John Brigg's answering machine in Connecticut.

Immediately, I wrote to David Peat to ask him to review my manuscript. In November 1995, before Thanksgiving, I called, and he said he had received my letter, but was busy finishing a manuscript and had not had time to write to me. He said he would read my manuscript as soon as he completed his book. I sent it just before Thanksgiving and waited. In early February, we spoke a couple of times, and he said the chapter explaining my healing method using the language of physics is clear. Unexpectedly, he offered to write the preface, although later the timing of publishing my book conflicted with the timing of his busy schedule, and he couldn't. Little did I know these synchronistic events were also important connections unfolding to my future soul mate.

Another spiritual synchronistic event had happened years earlier in 1987, when I was led to Father Flanagan's Boys Town, now Girls and Boys Town, Nebraska.

Father Flanagan's Boys Town, is an ecumenical home for boys and girls, and even though I am a Protestant, I was led there to share my healing method.

My former husband had a business meeting in Nebraska. We flew there on October 2, and that evening had dinner with some scientists and their wives. I was sharing my healing method with one of the wives, and she responded with great enthusiastic interest, and said that I might be interested in visiting Boys Town. I told her that I would love to go there and hadn't known where it was. She invited me to go to her house the next morning, as she had a friend flying in from Louisiana. She said we could go to lunch, and then visit Boys Town. When I arrived at her home, she introduced me to her friend, and then called her visiting friend's sister, and also invited her to lunch.

The wonderful spiritual coincidence further unfolded. At lunch the two sisters told me a very unexpected story—that they were the nieces of one of the first boys, Charles Kenworthy, to be taken into Boys Town. After lunch they drove me to Boys Town. We also visited the Boys Town museum where their uncle was honored as a great orator, who had given speeches to help raise money for Boys Town.

Because of this spiritual coincidence, I thought that I was being led to contact the Director to share my healing method. I was told that the director was Father Valentine Peter, and I wrote to him as soon as I returned to Los Angeles. I began sharing many ideas of my healing method with Father Peter through correspondence and my cassette tape for several years. This culminated in one of my prayers being published in the *Boys Town Prayer Book*[27] in1989. I am very grateful to Father Peter for his prayers, encouragement, and sharing ideas of this healing method with others.

Little did I know then, of the years of surprising twists and turns my path in life would take before God would lead me in an extraordinary way to meet and marry my soul mate. The next chapter begins that part of my spiritual path.

[18] Walsh, Anthony, *Science of Love*, (New York, Prometheus Books, 1991)

[19] *Ibid.*, p. 20

[20] *Ibid, p. 46*

[21] Peat, F. David, PhD, *Synchronicity: The Bridge Between Matter and Mind*, (New York, Bantam Books, 1987).

[22] *Ibid.*, p. 218.

[23] *Ibid.*

[24] Briggs, John, Ph.D, and Peat, F. David, Ph.D, *Turbulent Mirror*, (New York, Harper & Row Publishers, Inc., 1989).

[25] Peat, F. David, *The Philosopher's Stone: Chaos, Synchronicity, and the Hidden Order of the World*, (New York, Bantam Books, 1991)

[26] Teih, Mih, *The Classic and the Beautiful from the Literature of three Thousand Years*, (Joseph D. Carson, Philadelphia, Pa., 1901), Part 1, p. iii.

[27] *Boys Town Prayer Book*, (Nebraska, Father Flanagan's Home for Boys, 1989).

8. PLEASE TO COME TO WHERE I ARE

Love's Prayer

My Dearest, Special Twinkle Star
Please to come to where I are

Missing you deeply from afar
Life's full treasure together we are

Bountiful tree nest cradle's complete
Perfumed flowerbed eternally sweet

Our exultant hearts find calm retreat
Through touching moments when we meet

In arms our gentle souls entwine
Reaching, soaring heaven, being divine

Falling softly to love's deep sleep
We are the treasure safe to keep

(Written 1993)

Judy's Story

The morning of August 13, 1997, I went to work in the village (a half hour drive) and had what seemed an uneventful day. In the evening I was feeling deeply sad and lonely. Before falling asleep, I had an emergency talk with God. "You know that my soul mate hasn't been any of the men I've met since my divorce."

"I don't know where to go to find my soul mate. I have finished writing the manuscript on healing, and have done all the work you have asked me to do to help others, and feel too lonely to go on. Sometimes life had not been very pleasurable. Having a soul mate to discuss my writings about my healing method would be very helpful. Please bring him to me because I am too lonely, and feel that I can't do any more work for you until my soul mate is here."

The next morning when I opened my eyes, I felt much better. I told God that I understood that maybe there wasn't a soul mate for me, and that I would still go on and share this healing method with others.

That evening around 6 PM, I was hungry and wanted to cook my dinner. I also wanted to take a walk with my two dogs. I didn't know whether to go for my walk before my dinner or after. All of a sudden a clear message came *whispering* through my thoughts, "Drink two glasses of water, and take your two dogs to your favorite lake (a half-hour away). You'll meet some people, and be invited to dinner."

"God, are you sure?" This seemed bizarre—far-fetched, as this was a Thursday evening and *out in the middle of nowhere*. Since my one walk last January and a few walks in April, I had never met anyone on the way to the lake, or while there. This was now August. My son and I had walked there a week after his birthday party in April, and had taken a picture of a beautiful small lake with a willow tree for the cover of my book, and we sang songs while walking through the meadows. Now I wondered, "Is this another spiritual adventure, or just wishful thinking?"

Dressed in a woodsy shirt, oversized long shorts and a light pink baggy jacket, I was ready for my spiritual date that God seemed to have arranged. First I wanted my *healing method to be seen* and somewhat understood before I would let a future love relationship focus on me, so I *hid myself* underneath some very baggy hiking clothes. My dogs and I left on our unknown adventure, not sure whether I was in the land of wishful thinking. Maybe my loneliness had me making up stories of meeting someone in this isolated place—a pristine mirage! The excitement was building as we took each step up the path closer to the perhaps destined meeting place.

As soon as we arrived at the lake, one of my dogs splashed right into the lake. At first I couldn't believe my own eyes. Up on the hillside I saw two men walking down. Yes they were walking down the hillside, and then along the path beside the lake towards me. It's happening like I was told!

As many spiritual adventures I have been fortunate enough to experience, I am always amazed to watch another one unfold in front of me, as though for the first time. Holding the secret inside myself, I wondered what they might know and be thinking. I wondered which of the two men might be my soul mate, or would they lead me to him?

Tom's Story

For the past several years I had retreated into my shell in my cave in the city after my divorce, and was now just beginning to emerge again. Working late Wednesday evening, I arrived home after midnight, and found a phone message from my nephew, asking me to come to the mountains (a hundred miles away) that Thursday morning, August 14. He wanted me to help him save the flowers we had planted months before at my brother and sister-in-law's lake. He said there was an emergency. The water line we had previously laid had collapsed and the flowers were dying. This was the only time he could get there because he had an appointment Friday. He was bringing lots of food for us to eat Thursday night, and had to leave by dawn the next morning for his appointment. I had a Friday noon appointment so this was the only time possible for both of us. This brief window-in-time destined me for an unexpected meeting.

After not much sleep, Thursday morning I left a note at work and headed for the mountains early that morning. My nephew had arrived ahead of me so I began roaming the meadows and up the water line searching for him. When I finally found him, he had already cleared and relocated the entrance-sump of the water line in the creek and was rearranging the line down the gully. We worked all day getting the water to flow down this partially collapsed tube through a long narrow muddy cleft—a briar patch of stinging nettles and brambles, wild roses with thorns, slipping in the mud 500 feet back down to where it was still okay.

After a long frustrating day, we discovered in the late afternoon that my nephew had moved the headwater sump up too far, so we were 8 feet short and had no way of connecting to the final section. This meant going back and moving the sump and shifting the whole line back down again. We were not in the best of spirits—muddy, exhausted and in no mood for having company. I was extremely annoyed with the frustration and extra work. We finally finished around 6 PM and had saved the flowers. We began hiking back with our tools down past the lake heading for the cabin to cook something to eat.

As we cut across the hillside meadow, we noticed some dogs at the lake and thought my brother and his wife had come up with their dogs. As we approached closer we realized they were not their dogs. Then we saw what we thought was a trespasser, who from a distance looked like a man dressed in baggy clothing. Our irritation was building as my brother had recently had a problem with a trespasser damaging his property, so we detoured over to the lake to intercept him. We were sweaty, tired, and ready-to-fight—"fresh from the creeks, dog-dirty and loaded for bear!"[28]

Judy: My dogs were barking welcoming the new visitors. When they reached me, the nephew introduced himself as Glen (fictitious name), and his Uncle Tom who was standing some distance away befriending one of my dogs. Immediately, I noticed the light sparkling from Tom's eyes as he came closer. Glen did all the talking. He said they were up for the day fixing an irrigation problem. Glen said his Uncle Tom's brother and sister-in-law had rented this property for many years. We talked for a while about the property nearby, where I was living. Getting hungry, I finally said I needed to go home to make dinner. Immediately, Glen asked me to have dinner with them. He said they had brought a lot of extra food. Also, Tom emphasized that Glen had brought extra food, and they would enjoy my company. Since it had been whispered to me that I would meet some people and be invited to dinner, I comfortably accepted.

Tom: My attention was first focused on the barking Chow, which was approaching us. I was concerned because the dog was acting feisty and interposing. I calmed the dog down befriending her, and then noticed that instead of the male trespasser, it was a woman. My nephew was talking with her, and she turned out to be a neighbor living on an adjacent ranch.

Despite my initial feelings of unfriendliness, I felt a great sense of peace radiating from her as she looked calmly in my direction. I noticed her eyes seemed light gray in the early twilight shadows of the late afternoon. (A few weeks later, I remembered my grandfather had told me when he met my grandmother for the first time, he had noticed her eyes as being light gray.) She appeared to be observing from a distance this whole scene with an intelligent wisdom, as if she knew something we did not. She had a faint knowing smile. Glen introduced us. We talked briefly about the history of both ranches. We wanted to be friendly with this neighbor for my brother and sister-in-laws' sake. She then said she needed to go home and make dinner, and Glen immediately invited her to dinner. I said we have plenty of food, because Glen had brought extra food and was a gourmet cook.

Judy: Then Glen said his Uncle Tom is an optical physicist. Again, I almost felt struck by lightning. There I was very calm, and at the same time on the edge of peak excitement having to hold the secret inside myself of how I had been led there.

In 1995, I had such a wonderful experience by telephone with physicist David Peat, having a broad and varied background, who seemed to quickly understand my manuscript, and discoveries. I hoped that my soul mate would also have a broad background in physics and other subjects too. Over the years since my divorce, I had already discovered that I wasn't able to have a complete relationship with any man who didn't understand my method. I thought a soul mate with a broad background in physics would be able to easily understand my healing method more completely, thereby creating a closer bond. He would know who I am.

Not just anyone with a background in physics would have been able to understand. Someone with a very unique background was necessary, although I didn't spend any time dwelling on this. Standing there at the lake, I was observing the unfolding of the earlier whispers of this meeting with caution, and was careful to not tell what I had been told ahead of time.

As my excitement continued to build, I began sharing information about my manuscript with Tom. I told him about a physicist, F. David Peat, in London, who had read my manuscript, and had offered to write the preface for my book. Tom had heard of him, only hadn't read his books. He was interested in everything I had to say. I told him that I had made a number of discoveries, one of which is how I learned to more easily let go of unnecessary fear, pain, guilt and punishment from past memories, present situations and fear of the future. Through some language in physics is one way to metaphorically explain what I discovered, and how these discoveries may be working. Using an example of a frequency wave, when you focus on one particular emotion like universal grace-compassion, you may be resonating with one frequency wave and cannot occupy the space of another frequency wave (anti-grace). Also when others may not be living that concept, they may not be occupying that particular frequency wave. What does this mean? It means that when you may be in the state of grace, although others are not, you may be protected.

On July 11, just a month before, I had mailed my manuscript to an agent and was in a waiting period of six weeks to hear the results. Tom told me he understood this process because his mother, as a writer had often endured these typical manuscript approval delays. He said his mother had written many young people's books. I had not heard of them, and was interested in knowing about them and her life.

They walked me up to their cabin, and Tom began lighting the oil lamps because the cabin had no electricity. Glen began preparing a gourmet dinner on an old fashioned wood-burning stove while we all gaily talked together. We had an inspiring, mystical evening lit with oil lamp lights in the window sills, on the fireplace, on the table, the harpsichord and kitchen sink. We shared enlivening conversation. I told them about the illness I had in 1984, and how I had healed, even though at the time I didn't want to heal. (The details of the healing method are in Chapter 17.)

I talked more about my healing method, and that I had discovered messages that seemed to have been or be confused, missing, and/or hidden from what I call the menu in my mind and other people's, like on a computer. I think that this may have kept many people trapped in a problem called "double binds" (mental/emotional traps) making it difficult to let go of unnecessary depression, fear, pain, and guilt, or even discovering how.

Brief description of some double binds

Anthropologist Gregory Bateson and colleagues first acknowledged the double bind in 1956. In a double bind, you might have had conflicting choices or demands, and it seemed that no matter which choice you made, you would lose. You may not have seen the wisdom of your possible choices, or not seen any healthy alternatives. In addition, you may have felt wrong, bad, mad or guilty, or felt and thought you were punished even for correct perceptions. Bateson said many children have been torn by conflicting input.

One of the ways I describe an example of a double bind is:

1. People may have not felt safe because of experiences of fear, pain, and guilt.

2. Then they may not have felt safe to let go of the unnecessary fear, pain, and guilt, because that fear, pain, and guilt itself, which caused them to distance themselves from others for protection—may have created an illusion of safety.

Knowingly or not, they may have thought that remembering the old fear and pain may have caused them to keep their distance, and hoped that new fear and pain would not happen again. It may be that *remembering the actual information* (the facts) connected to what caused the fear and pain, rather than the actual fear and pain that can be an aid in prevention.

Sometimes emotions of fear, pain, and guilt may have overloaded a person, numbing their other protective senses which may have made even knowing and making wise and healthy choices difficult, or hampered their ability to stick with them.

The interwoven problems of "double binds" with other contradictions in language and logic may explain why many people were unable to let go of fear and pain easily or at all. This may have affected their ability to have a healthy self-worth, as well as how to think, feel, and behave constructively all the time—they couldn't figure out how.

Also, I discovered another problem and answer of how we may have been influenced by contradictory messages related to acquiring knowledge and wisdom which may be a part of the "collective *sub*conscious," as I call it, (rather than "collective *un*conscious"). These influences came from myths and stories from ancient history. This double bind may have shown itself when you felt guilty for knowing or learning too much. This has also prevented many from having a healthy self-esteem. How?

1. Some have been taught that on the one hand, they were wrong to be wise, know too much, and . . .
2. . . . on the other hand that they were only 100% valuable when they knew it all (a confusing contradiction).

Statements like, "Don't be nosy, mind your own business, have faith—don't ask questions, and curiosity killed the cat" are some of the confusing messages that were communicated.

My book, *A Path to Light*, includes many other contradictions and interwoven binds, and work sheets and evaluation form that may aid you in solving some mental/emotional traps. These forms are also in this book in the Appendix: Preventive and Healing Kit.

The following are a few of the missing or hidden messages that you may use in dealing with some traps:

1. *"I am always safe knowing and living truth when healthy for me."*

This may be an aid in awakening yourself to see, hear, speak and write when it is safe, healthy, and wise for you.

(I added:—*"when healthy for me"* to the above message and all the others to give extra time to ask, "What, where and when is healthy for me and others?" before making choices.)

2. *"I am always safe not hurting myself, you, or others when healthy for me."*

This key positive phrase means you may be providing yourself with a new aura of safety.

Also, *"when healthy for me,"* allows for the times when you may receive or give some pain whenever saying no to something unwise and unhealthy. An example is when there is some short-term pain in saying **"no"** to an unwise and unhealthy choice, or instead you might feel comforted.

After reflection, I realized that this whole statement *is* the state of grace and compassion. This message seems to have been missing from, or hidden and confused in the computer of many people's minds. The questions are why and how? Some detailed answers are addressed in my book, *A Path to Light.* Further, when the above concept is accepted, you may become better able to let go of unnecessary fear, pain, and guilt.

> *You are protecting yourself looking from a different perspective—one of safety.*

When you don't hurt yourself or others, and when you don't allow others to hurt you (when it is healthy for you), you may experience a new form of safety. Not hurting yourself or others means you are *safe to not receive or give pain when healthy for you.* Then you may further let go of your pain, (which may have been a defense, real or imagined) by focusing on the additional thought:

> *3.* "I am always safe letting go of fear, pain, guilt and punishment with (whomever) when healthy for me."

Also, *"when healthy for me"* may aid you in still maintaining awareness and respect for potential hazards. You may prevent hurting yourself or others (or as much), as well as further let go of unnecessary fear, pain, and guilt by the following . . .

4. *"I am always safe receiving and giving grace, compassion, love and peace to myself and to _____ when healthy for me,"*

With this loving thought *you may defuse your anger, and/or diminish your sadness, as well as that of others* to some degree. Additionally, when you are busy sending out good-will thoughts to others, you may be protected from receiving the full impact of any destructive thoughts. I did this even in situations of potential anger or violence, and then had the peace of mind to know what action to take. It is important to assess each situation.

Repeatedly focusing on the four above messages, along with other messages, allowed me to quickly dissolve my fear, pain, and guilt. Remembering that you or others may be trapped in mental/emotional traps may make it easier to also remember that you don't need to take personally others' painful words or actions whether they actually intended them or not. You may avoid adding to your pain or theirs by the following:

You may prevent yourself from receiving their fear and pain by *silently* receiving and giving them grace, compassion, love and peace. People in pain may be really seeking this whether they are aware of it or not, and just may not know how to feel comfortable with comfort, safety, and love. When you are busy sending out the above good will thought, you may not receive as much, or any of others' ill will.

At the time I began using this healing method, I didn't have any faith, belief, or the will to live, nor was I able to completely *feel* the concepts of grace and compassion. My fear and pain were blocking. I could focus on grace and compassion; yet not completely feel them at that time. The concepts made logical sense to me that this is wise to think and do. This means I am creating the space and planting the seeds for myself, you and others to be well—creating in my mind the space for potential healing by radiating harmony to others—not adding to destructive thought patterns in myself or others. This may also work in situations of potential or actual violence.

After discussing my healing method, I asked Glen to please call me, and let me know when he got any good results from some of the ideas I was sharing. I noticed that Tom was actually interpreting some aspects of my method for Glen. I was very touched by Tom's telling me that he had been depressed for some periods in his life, only he did want to see how things would turn out. He said that his mother had mentioned to him that his father had always had that attitude. His father had passed away when Tom was 8 years old.

Tom: Our conversation flowed easily and joyfully. I was surprised when she began to talk about physics. We also talked about her manuscript on healing, health foods and many other topics. During the evening, I found myself at first thinking of her as very naive with her good-will approach to healing. As our conversation progressed, I was fascinated and interested, although skeptical. I noticed she was able to intelligently defend against our every criticism, and she was the originator of some interesting ideas and language. The title she gave me sounded maybe meaningful—maybe buzz words, although I didn't know completely what they meant. Maybe some professionals had fed her a line of complicated jargon, which she was parroting. She sounded poetic anyhow. My curiosity was piqued. I wanted to understand what she was talking about. After more in-depth conversation during and after dinner, I found myself defending and interpreting what I understood of her method to Glen. Then it was time to walk her home.

---

28   Dan McGrew, Sam McGee: The Poems of Robert Service, *The Shooting of Dan McGrew*, Stonesong Press, Inc., 1987, (New York, Barnes&Noble Books, 1996) p. 57

Somewhere in Time

Somewhere lingering whispering time
Your traveling mind now meets mine

Solving ancient riddles, in happiness we unwind
Releasing the puzzle of universal hidden binds

Floating freely, air whispering secrets of truth
Wisdom now soaring, saving blessed youth

Dancing on clouds, forming images of mirth
Universal compassion, blanketing all births

Sprinkling star dust, singing heavens of the mind
Now together freely, lost somewhere in time

Blissfully humming, expanding, traversing the climb
Always sharing, cherishing somewhere in time

(Written 1993)

9. ILLUMINATING MOONLIGHT

JUDY: AROUND 10:30 PM, Glen and Tom walked me home along the uneven forest path. We weaved in and out of pure reflection with dancing moon shadows among the trees on a warm, close to full-moon evening. The path was very uneven. Glen said he would take one of my arms, and told Tom to take my other arm. Tom took my hand instead. Eventually the ground became a little more even, smoothing our way, and Tom still held my hand. Glen let go of my arm to take a swing on an old tire hanging from a tree. I felt embarrassed that Tom was still holding my hand, and to ease my uncomfortable feelings, I reminded myself that Tom was unfamiliar with this area, and I didn't want him to fall. The path soon would be rough again so I held on, too. I was glad my shyness could hide in the shadows of the trees.

As we walked, we talked and laughed. Again we talked about the unusual complicated happenings at the ranch—of new owners appearing, present owners disappearing, and the former owner coming back, with the caretaker and his wife leaving just two weeks before. Tom said this reminded him of a story he read in a science fiction magazine years ago.

The story is of a philosopher and friend who were earnestly discussing mind and matter—various deep philosophical theories of reality and existence. He presented the egoist concept that reality was just a construct of his mind, arguing that "All these items around us are just a figment of my imagination. If I didn't believe in them, they would cease to exist."

He continued arguing with his friend, becoming more certain of his theory. When he discussed his doubts about the mere *things* about him, *some* items nearby actually disappeared—Poof! Then more and more! Finally, the philosopher paused, and said with alarm: "Hey, maybe—, maybe even I *myself* am a mere figment of my *own* imagi—...", and Poof!—He disappeared, too!

We went laughing into my house talking about who was going to appear or disappear next, as they had just appeared unexpectedly into my life out in the middle of nowhere. They stayed and talked for another hour. Last April, I had taken some pictures of the lake where we met earlier in the evening. Coincidentally, I was planning to use it for the cover of my book, and showed them the pictures.

Before Tom and Glen left, Tom asked me to repeat the title of my healing method when I had applied for a research grant. I said, "A Dissociative Method to Release Psychobiologic Binds." He said, "How poetic!" and wrote it down—"But just what does it mean?" he asked.

My healing method may give tools to dissociate—separate from—let go of unnecessary fear, pain, guilt, and/or numbness from memories. Through using my Self-worth Exercise worksheet (pp. 236-241), you may discover and release yourself from many double binds (mental/emotional traps) that have affected you. Instead of reinforcing the traps and old painful feelings through repeated expression of old feelings, you may release them in a new way. Repetition of new specific thoughts that address these old traps and feelings in a unique way, may allow you to let go. Through a form of disuse, the old feelings may disappear.

Without repression, you may interrupt the old feelings often enough, with somewhat similar, yet different overlapping new constructive thoughts—you may further free yourself. It is like a train switching tracks at a junction, and then traveling on a new track with new interpretations, and language. Only the former track of painful feelings disappears. (I still retained my memories, but without the unnecessary fear, pain, guilt, or numbness.) New constructive feelings appear, along with some former repressed constructive feelings.

Back in 1991, I had been interested in finding grant money to do a research project demonstrating results of my healing method with Viet Nam Veterans having Post Traumatic Stress Disorder (PTSD). These are people still suffering from painful flashbacks from their war experiences. It had been suggested that I contact George Solomon, M.D., psychiatrist, an expert on PTSD and psychoneuroimmunology (mind and emotions affecting the immune system). He was then at the Veteran's Hospital, in the San Fernando Valley, and Professor of Psychiatry at the University of California at Los Angeles (UCLA). I contacted him for copies of his published research.

In 1992, when the Office of Alternative Medicine was offering grants, I applied and Dr. Solomon, Dr. Baron and others became my consultants on a research grant application to test my healing method with cancer patients. Dr. Solomon assisted me with choosing a title for my research project after I described my healing method—the above "poetic" title. Also, he suggested research papers by other people, and offered me the use of his library with his unique collection of books on Viet Nam Veterans and psychoneuroimmunology. After the 1993 Northridge earthquake, that destroyed the Veteran's Hospital, he quickly set up psychological and immunological tests to document the post-earthquake stress-effects on the employees. He published the useful results in a paper titled "Shaking Up Immunity."[29] Sometime after the earthquake, Dr. Solomon moved to UCLA where he was Professor Emeritus of Psychiatry and Biobehavioral Sciences. Recently in 1997, he published "Immune and Nervous System Interactions,"[30] an analytical bibliography and commentary of 528 references.

(Coincidently, I had presented public seminars at a nearby Psychiatric Hospital 3 years before the earthquake. One of the women (60 years old) learned to overcome her many panic attacks. In 1993, she experienced the big Northridge earthquake, living nearby—yet remained calm during and after the destructive quake.)

The fact that some messages are missing or hidden from the consciousness of many people explains why, even when they knew what was good for them, they did not choose that path, or when on it for a while, they quit. The following is an example:

Maintain Healthy Habits?

One of the problems many have experienced is how to maintain new healthy habits. For example: Research studies demonstrate that relaxation and exercise programs benefit general health and the immune system (and thereby resistance to disease) in young and old.[31, 32, 33]

However, a *significant observation* in one such study was made in a later follow-up on a group of subjects who had definitely benefited from such a program [i.e., had shown improved measures of immune function, and had spontaneously reported being much more aware and enjoyed the program]. Researchers noted that later, surprisingly, only a quarter of them "reported setting aside regular periods of time for relaxation such as they had during the training period."[34]

EVEN THOUGH IT'S GOOD FOR YOU

The problem in *any new healthy program* seems to be how to continue doing it, even though it's good for you!

> Come, there's no use in crying like that!" said
> Alice to herself, rather sharply, "I advise you to
> leave off this minute!" She generally *gave herself
> very good advice* (though she *very seldom followed it*),
> and sometimes she scolded herself so severely as to
> bring tears into her eyes . . .[35]

With the healing method I discovered, you can safely add new thought processes so you may resolve conflicts, solve some double binds (mental/emotional traps), more easily let go of unnecessary fear and pain, and make many more healthy enjoyable choices. You then may control and transform your thoughts, feelings and behavior—your responses to stress in the present in a more effective and harmonious manner. Then you can focus on the thought, *"I receive and give myself healthy advice, and I follow it,"* and may get the results. This allows you to enjoy being self-motivated to do what is healthy for you (follow wise, healthy advice), so then you want to and *do continue.*

Focusing on a Pulse

In addition to focusing on the messages of the relaxation exercise of my healing method, intuitively, I chose to focus on a pulse in different areas of my body. This was as if I had a telephone hookup to all parts of my body and could ring them up at will. I silently repeated, "I'm always safe feeling my pulse in and around _____." I was imagining "sending" healing twinkle star cells and "disappearing" the cells causing the pain, stiffness and swelling. I did this without any faith, belief or hope that this would work. I did have faith that I was safe to die naturally.

Because of so much physical and emotional pain, I was not in a relaxed state. Also, I was unable to take any anti-inflammatory drugs because of being allergic. I simply had an attitude of experimentation, and wanted to die without emotional pain if at all possible. (See details on pp. 73-74.)

Every two hours I would do the half-hour relaxation exercise focusing on these thoughts, even though I couldn't relax. When not doing the exercise, I would continue to focus on these thoughts throughout the day by persistent repetition. Sometimes I got very tired of doing this.

Then I would take short breaks, and remind myself that I had been spending a lot of time and energy thinking painful thoughts, so I might as well use the same time and energy thinking the new harmonious thoughts. Before falling asleep at night, I would repeat the messages 4 times. Day after day I continued this pattern, because it increasingly seemed to make sense.

Tom seemed very interested in my discussion about my method. It was getting late, so he and Glen both hugged me and left. One of my dogs named "Sunshine" walked them back home. I was happy she did because she would probably protect them from snakes along the forest path.

Jewels

Crystals tinkling, bird songs, drifting
    beyond my longing ears
Tingling warm tender breezes, caressing
    softly, my silken hair
Lofty luminous clouds, playing
    images through whispering air
Dazzling sunbeams radiance, glowing
    for everyone, everywhere
Shimmering moonlight, loving quiescence,
    illuminating those free to care
Twinkling star dust shower, sprinkling tidings,
    Enlightening grace to share
Sparkling wondrous Jewels in air, bringing
    gently I to You, You to Me
Passing treasured moments in time,
    everywhere, returning us to see
Revealing the way to the place of Grace,
    anticipating not where it is to be
Looking deep within, releasing all that is kind,
    enjoying loving you and me

(Written 1993)

Tom: Then it was time to walk Judy home. We continued talking with her all the way home. I felt so comfortable that we could talk so easily about so many varied subjects that when we arrived at her house I became oblivious to the time. She brought out pictures she had taken that April of the lake where Glen and I had worked so hard landscaping and planting flowers where we had just met her at 6:20 PM. I thought this was special, and an unusual coincidence that she really appreciated the lake enough to take a picture of it and wanted to use it for the cover of her book. Glen hugged her as we left, so I felt comfortable to do the same.

We began walking home and noticed that Judy's dog, Sunshine was with us. We tried to shoo her home, but she insisted on escorting us to our cabin. Glen thought it was just as well because she was probably protecting us from snakes. He began to describe all the different varieties around here and where they might be. Sunshine still wouldn't go home and spent the night on the porch. We needed to get up very early to leave the next morning, but slept well past dawn. Glen realized that he would not be able to make his distant appointment. We went to check our new water sprinklers at the lake and Sunshine stayed with us. Then we went back to the house and began making breakfast.

Judy: The next morning I found Tom had left his little flashlight on my living room table, and my dog, Sunshine hadn't returned. (More things appearing and disappearing). I walked up to their house and there was Sunshine. Tom and Glen invited me to eat breakfast with them, another delightful memory. I shared more information about the healing method and mentioned that in my manuscript, I had quoted an idea that I didn't agree with by philosopher Ludwig Wittgenstein. Tom asked me whether I knew of Mary Shelly, who was married to the poet Shelley and had written *Frankenstein*. He said she was a relative of Wittgenstein. I didn't know of her, and went on to tell them what the philosopher Wittgenstein had written.

> For an answer which cannot be expressed the
> question too cannot be expressed—*the riddle*
> *d*oes not exist . . .[36]

Because of the interwoven nature of multiple double binds, and my own language problems, a number of riddles had been so hidden that it had been impossible for me to form the appropriate questions to unlock their answers. Therefore, it appeared that the riddle did not exist. However, because of an unexpected circumstance in my life (facing death), I had an opportunity to shift my perspective into a different frame of reference, which gave me a unique opportunity to be *safe to notice* some previously hidden contradictions and riddles. This safety made it possible for me to ask related questions and receive useful answers. In Chapter 17: Path to Discovery (pp. 201-229), I describe this experience.

Wittgenstein did say that maybe the great problems in Philosophy are no more than pseudo-problems brought about by the lack of attention to language. He also said, "Don't ask what a word means, ask how it is used," mentioned in Physicist, F. David Peat's book, "Pathways of Chance," p. 69.

An important aspect of my method includes the concept: "We are always safe being together, when healthy for us," and also includes an explanation of what that means, as well as how we are safe.

In addition to: "I am always safe not hurting myself or others when healthy for us," I focus on:

"I am, you and all people are always safe.

This is not a "Pollyanna" idea. Just because the above statement itself may temporarily seem untrue, does not mean it *is* untrue! Some people have said to me, "I may be safe and you may be safe. Don't tell me all people are safe." Even though you have experienced a lack of safety, dreaded some future experience, or real or imagined threats, you can change your point of view. You may create safety in what may seem or be a potentially unsafe situation, (protect yourself in and from unsafe situations) by having and acting on clearer perceptions. In my mind, I thought I was also projecting safety onto others (creating a safety field). Everyday, we pass by people who may be potentially unsafe, but are still safe. There is a form of self-protection in concentrating on "We are always safe, when healthy for us," explained in Chapter 17: Path of Discovery (pp. 203-205).

Well, it was time for me to go to work, and Tom and Glen also needed to drive back to the city. Glen told me that Tom's brother and sister-in-law would be visiting here tomorrow and to return and introduce myself. It was time for me to go home and get ready to leave for my job, so I left not knowing when we would meet again.

Tom: Suddenly, Judy showed up at the kitchen door searching for Sunshine, and Sunshine greeted her in the kitchen. She had brought back my favorite flashlight. We invited her to have breakfast with us, and continued to have a very delightful conversation. When she was referring to a quote by the philosopher Wittgenstein that she had in her manuscript, I made a mistaken comment that his daughter was Mary Shelly who wrote "Frankenstein" and was the wife of the poet Shelley. I had confused the philosopher Wittgenstein with the English philosopher Godwin who actually was her father (an error perhaps triggered by the similarity of "Wittgenstein" to "Frankenstein" and her middle name after her mother, "Wollstonecraft"). Also, I neglected to tell her that one of the books my mother wrote was *Shelley's Mary*.[37] This is why I had the information even though I had it mixed up as I later realized. Judy had to leave for work, and I needed to get back to give a ride to a friend at noon. Also, I had a date that night with someone visiting from out of town.

I drove back to the city. That evening with my date, we seemed to have a lot in common and easily talked together. However, during our time together talking, I found myself quoting and explaining using points Judy had made in sharing her healing method with me. Interestingly, I began to notice my differences with my date in our basic values and recognized this was not the best relationship for me. I actually was comparing her to Judy. We parted diplomatically that weekend.

Judy: On Saturday, in the late afternoon, something told me that it was time for me to walk back to the enchanting house to meet Tom's brother and sister-in-law. When I got there, they had just arrived in their car, and invited me to sit and talk with them. They were very kind, wrote down my phone number, and said they would invite me to dinner in the future.

[29]   Solomon, George, F., MD, Segerstrom, Suzanne C., MA, Grohr, Peter, MD, Kemeny, Margaret, PhD, and Fahey, John, MD, "Shaking Up Immunity: Psychological and Immunologic Changes After a Natural Disaster," *Psychosomatic Medicine, 1997,* 59:114-127.

[30]   Solomon, G., MD, "Immune & Nervous System Interactions," Fund for Psychoneuroimmunology, Malibu, CA, July 1997.

[31]   Solomon, George, MD; Fiatarone, Maria; Benton, Donna; Morley, John; Bloom, Eda; Makinodan, Takashi; "Psychoimmunologic and Endorphin Function in the Aged," *Annals of the New York Academy of Sciences,* March 29, 1988, Vol. 521.

[32]   Fiatarone, Maria; Morley, John; Bloom, Eda; Benton, Donna; Solomon, George; Makinodan, Takashi; "The Effect of Exercise on Natural Killer Cell Activity in Young and Old Subjects," *Journal of Gerontology: MEDICAL SCIENCES,* 1989, Vol. 44, No. 2, M37-45.

[33]   Kiecolt-Glaser, Janice; Glaser, Ronald; et al; "Psychosocial Enhancement of Immunocompetence in a Geriatric Population," 1985, *Health Psychology.* 4: 24-41.

[34]   *Ibid.*, p. 39.

[35]   Carroll, Lewis, *Alice's Adventures in Wonderland,* Compiled & Arranged by Cooper Edens, (New York, Bantam Books, 1989, p 21.

[36]   Wittgenstein, Ludwig, *Tractatus Logico-Philosophicus,* (New York: Humanities Press, 1951), p. 187.

[37]   Leighton, Margaret, *Shelley's Mary,* 1973, (New York, Farrar, Straus and Giroux, 1973).

10. RETURN TO SANTA MONICA

JUDY: ON SUNDAY AFTERNOON, I left for Los Angeles
to visit my daughter for her birthday. Monday morning I was
in the Santa Monica Library. I began to fill with excitement as
I had experienced other wonderful coincidences here through
books that had led me to the physicist, F. David Peat. I typed
Tom's mother's name and many titles of books appeared. I
began reading rapidly. I came to the title *Shelley's Mary, The
Life of Mary Godwin Shelley*.[38] Tom had not mentioned that
his mother had written this book. He had only told me about
Mary Shelley, the author of *Frankenstein*, being a relative of
Wittgenstein, and that she was married to the poet Shelly. My
excitement was rewarded.

Godwin was my grandparents' name, so maybe this was a
distant relative of mine. Tom had not mentioned Godwin when
he had told me about Mary Shelley. Then I came to the title
Judith of France.[39] Since my name is Judith and recalling my
memorable visits to France, my attention was totally captured.
Tom had not mentioned this book at all. The memory of my
Fleur-de-lis lily pin came back to me.

I left the library and began reading *Shelley's Mary* first. After
reading it, I realized that maybe Tom had been mistaken about
Wittgenstein being a relative of Mary Shelley. Her father,
William Godwin, was also a philosopher, and maybe Tom was
confused, because Mary wrote *Frankenstein*, which sounded
similar to Wittgenstein. After reading some of *Shelley's Mary*, I
thought that Tom's mother was an exciting author.

My daughter and I met and enjoyed a wonderful celebration
of her birthday for several days.

As soon as I finished reading *Shelley's Mary*, I began to read
Judith of France and was astounded by the similarities of her

mission in life to mine! Judith was great-granddaughter to Charlemagne, and daughter to King Charles the Bald of France. In 856 AD, her father selected the aged King Aethelwulf of England, against Judith's wishes, for her to marry. This was to gain wealth and lands in England for France. Charles knew that Aethelwulf would not live long because of his age and ailing health.

Judith's father was the child of Emperor Louis and the young Empress Judith, a second marriage. This marriage was the cause for so much strife, hatred and wars because Emperor Louis took back lands which he had previously given to his older grown sons (although sealed by solemn oaths and treaties) in order to provide for his new youngest son by his young, second wife Judith. Family jealousies then were responsible for the strife and wars between countries involving innocent people such as we have seen in our lifetime.

The Archbishop Hincmar told Judith of this history and warned her because of her name also being Judith. He said that between her father's Franks and Louis's Germans, they had created a realm, Lothaire's land, which some were calling Lorraine, and that Louis's Judith was blamed for tearing apart a family and thereby a nation!

He thought that Judith of France's path was predestined, with Heaven having already marked her path because her name was also Judith. This would remind others of her grandmother Judith, who had been the cause of so much trouble. He felt her only course was to be humble, and hope for the Holy Saints to intercede to turn God's wrath away from her.

Judith finally went to see her wise tutor, a priest, John Scotus Erigena. He counseled her instead, with a positive approach, and said the following:

> The Archbishop is a great prince of the Church. It is perhaps presumptuous of me, a poor lay scholar, to deny the truth of what he has told you. Yet in this one thing he is mistaken! he said, firmly. 'A

just and wrathful God? Bah! The words contradict themselves, for doesn't wrath always distort judgment? And never could God, whom we know to be infinitely just and merciful, foredoom any land or any soul! To believe that would be to imply vengeful cruelty to Heaven, and that would be a blasphemous contradiction indeed!

Heaven marks no paths for us, Princess,' he said. We must choose our own, guided by such intelligence and good will, as we possess. Yes, every human soul while it lives and breathes has some freedom to choose its way, even if it lies only between life and death.

At every turn in your road you will have choices to make between good and evil. Even though you mistake the way and choose wrongly, never despair. Always believe that you will be given another chance, as truly as God is merciful and understanding!

It must be renewed constantly in your heart with all the strength and new discernment—yes, and courage—that experience in life can bring you![40]

In order for Judith to not inherit the hatred and strife of her grandmother Judith, she now had her mission to never cause strife between father and son, nor brother and brother, thereby nations. She carried this oath in a locket around her neck. The King Aethelwulf, her future husband, said that this might mean peace and mercy for us all.

This is very similar to my own mission to share this healing method through my book *A Path to Light* and this book. My books show *a way to receive and give universal grace, compassion, love and peace to oneself and everyone.*

In *A Path to Light*, some barriers are presented that explain why so many people have had difficulty making healthy choices (knowingly or unknowingly), as well as how to let go of, or go through these barriers to make many more wise choices. The potential of this method is to end unnecessary strife and hatred that in some cases has been perpetuated for centuries.

Also, it is interesting that John Scotus emphasized in 856 AD the need to renew "constantly" a dedication to peace. This is another similarity that I also encourage people to daily repeat the aspects of my healing method. *Daily repetition* is as important as the messages themselves in order to gain and keep the results.

Finding the philosophy of my healing method expressed by Tom's mother through Judith and John Scotus, including the need to constantly reaffirm the message to keep it actively alive affected me deeply at many different levels.

1. the spiritual coincidence of Judith's message to never cause strife between father and son and brother with brother and thence their nation, which is similar in my message of grace-compassion for one's self, family and all people.

2. the act of Judith writing her message on a piece of parchment and keeping it in a locket around her neck. This is similar to my having written the manuscript, A Path to Light, and having the messages put on a small card for people to carry with them and use everywhere.

3. "renew constantly—the dedication to peace"—the need to repeat the messages through my relaxation exercise, during physical exercise, in music, poetry and written reminders for people.

4. that we have free will to choose between good and evil, and even when she may have chosen wrongly, she was given another chance because of God's mercy. One of the points of my healing method is that grace—forgiveness, mercy, and compassion are to be lived within yourself and between yourself and others in order to heal.

5. Another powerful spiritual connection for me was that after Judith stayed true to her course of peace, eventually she was rescued by her soul mate, from her self-imposed isolation, despair and possible death, thereby saving both of them.

Was this to give me hope that I, on my continued road dedicated to peace, no matter what, was finally to meet my soul mate—someone who truly could understand the healing method—rescue me from my own self-imposed isolation because of working on the manuscript? Was this to be Tom? Would we save each other, or would he lead me to my soul mate?

What is different about my mission and Judith of France's mission is that she may have thought that others would learn just through her example. There may have been the thought that through her model others would change, and yet they did not. My mission is an addendum to Judith of France in sharing with all people *how to be* in the state of grace and compassion all the time,—*what* some of the barriers are, and *how to release them.*

Overwhelmed with increasing excitement, I wanted to speak with Tom—let him know of these spiritual coincidences with his mother's books, and my own life, but I didn't know how to reach him.

[38] Leighton, Margaret, *Shelley's Mary, The Life of Mary Godwin Shelley*, (New York, Farrar, Straus and Giroux, 1973).

[39] Leighton, Margaret, *Judith of France*, (Boston, Houghton Mifflin Co., Boston, The Riverside Press, Cambridge, 1948).

[40] *Ibid.*, p. 52.

11. WONDERING PATH

JUDY: AFTER CELEBRATING MY daughter's birthday for a few days, I returned home and finished reading the book *Judith of France*. By the following Saturday I wrote a note to Tom, and walked to the house near the lake. I left my note on the door with the hope that someone would come soon and pass the note to Tom. The next day I walked back and got the note thinking that in my excitement I had written too much. I was concerned that it might be too overwhelming for him to read. On Sunday, I rewrote the note, and again walked back leaving it on the door of the house near the lake.

Tuesday morning I still felt uncomfortable that I may have said too much about the synchronistic events with Tom's mother's books. Again, I walked back to get my note. I thought that these synchronistic stories may be better to tell him in person.

On the way back, I met a young boy on the forest path. He was near the isolated empty cabin. Last January while searching for my lost cat, I had wondered whether someone there would lead me to my soul mate. He said that his grandparents owned this property, and they would be arriving in the afternoon. Our meeting took so long, that I didn't have enough time to walk to the house to retrieve my note, and then get to work on time. I thought that in the afternoon, I would walk back there, get my note, and ask the young boy's grandparents for Tom's brother's phone number. If they didn't know the phone number, I would write a more simple note to leave at the house again.

Coincidentally, when I returned home from work, I had received a message on my answering machine from Tom's sister-in-law inviting me to dinner on the following Saturday. When she left her phone number, the last 4 digits had been cut off, so I was unable to return her call.

In the late afternoon, around 5 PM I walked back towards the lake, and met the grandparents. After some conversation, I explained that Tom's sister-in-law had just left a message on my machine, but the last four digits of her phone number had been cut off. When I asked them if they had her phone number, they said they hadn't brought it with them. They said they would call her when they arrived home the next day and ask her to call me. Then they suggested I call information because they thought she was listed. Again I went back and retrieved my note, and after returning home, I called information. Luckily, I had the first three digits of the phone number to verify because there were three other listings with the same last name. The operator found the right number for me, and now my excitement grew again. Right away I called her, and she said that Tom was also coming to dinner, and then I could tell him all the news related to his mother's books and connections to my life.

Tom: I got back to work and a very hectic schedule to make up for my time in the mountains, car problems and a busy weekend. On Tuesday, two weeks later, there was a message on my machine from my sister-in-law. She was asking me to come to the mountains Friday night to get up early on Saturday morning to help my brother cut wood. I thought I might have a chance to walk down and see that neighbor lady again.

Friday night I was working late, so I drove up Saturday morning. They had mentioned that their grandson and friends would also be there for dinner and Judy was looking forward to seeing me. Because she mentioned Judy's name along with different friends and relatives, and I had mis-remembered Judy's name, I was not prepared for whom I was to meet. When Judy and I were introduced two weeks before, I was mesmerized by her eyes, and was not paying close attention to her name. I didn't know this was the Judy I was coming to see again. When my nephew and Judy were talking about the owner of the property where Judy lives, I thought I heard some other name. When my sister-in-law mentioned Judy, I didn't realize this was the person I had already met, and was hoping to meet again, maybe on Sunday.

Judy: By Saturday the electricity in the air was so high, I could hardly stand it myself. It reminded me of the night I went to Lambeth Palace, and other spiritual adventures. I did everything I could to dissipate the energy. Earlier in the day I was out with my son looking at a house I was thinking of buying. By the late afternoon, I was calmer with a moderate amount of excitement beginning to overflow again by 6 PM.

Our meeting felt so mystical again. We talked for hours while we were provided with food and the privacy to begin getting to know each other. I told Tom about celebrating my daughter's birthday the previous weekend, and finding and reading his mother's books. Then I shared how significant they are to my life.

The book, *Shelley's Mary, The Life of Mary Godwin Shelley*[41] had caught my attention because my grandparents' name is Godwin. Then I told him about *Judith of France*,[42] and the connection to my manuscript and healing method. Tom didn't remember all the details of *Judith of France*. He wanted to see my manuscript, which I had brought, and began looking through it reading some sections. Later, adorned with a warm starlit night, outside we joined with the other guests, and had a most joyful dinner. I invited everyone to visit for lunch the next day. Only Tom and another guest said they would.

Tom: Early Saturday evening, I was resting on the couch near a window from a day of cutting wood when a car drove up. I raised myself up to look out the window. At that moment, I realized that this Judy invited to dinner was the person that I had met and hoped to meet again. I had mistakenly heard a different name when we were introduced.

After Judy arrived, we were sent out on the porch to talk, and brought hors d'oeuvres. Looking back, it seems that all the others were kept busy with preparations or otherwise occupied so we could talk undisturbed. We talked for several hours before dinner. Judy told me about her adventures in Santa Monica with my mother's books, and I asked to see her manuscript that she had brought. I was very moved by her consulting in hospitals to help others let go of their pain. I had been involved in doing some volunteer work in hospitals. I felt like I had always known Judy and always would—a total feeling of comfort. After dinner, a friend and I sat talking with Judy at the dining table all lit with oil lamps till just past midnight animated like children. Some relatives and friends were already asleep on the living room couches, some in sleeping bags on the floor and others were still sitting outside talking. Earlier in the evening Judy had invited me and everyone else to lunch the next day. Another friend and I were the only ones who could go. Judy said she needed to go home and began leaving. I was figuring out how to hug her again which I did. She left and I looked forward to the lunch the next day.

Judy: The next day Tom arrived, and we spent some time working on a paper I needed help with editing. Soon the other guest arrived and we had lunch together. Tom's friend had to leave early to go back to the city, so Tom drove him back to the house and then returned after some time. We spent the afternoon talking, and then I asked him whether he would like to go for a hike up into my mystical meadow in the forest. He said yes, and off we went. As we walked so many beautiful wild flowers seemed to be floating above the ground. The flowers reminded me of what my healing method allows to happen, and a poem I love that describes this experience. One of the results that happens when using my healing method is when you let go of the fear and pain from the past, you find more than was lost. There are nurturing memories and feelings that were covered over (blocked) and now can be felt. My daughter had shared the poem with me many years ago when she was in college. In my seminars and private consultations, I share e.e cummings poem "when faces called flowers float out of the ground,"[43] and I began to quote it for Tom.

when more than was lost has been found, has been found

As we entered, the glowing mystical meadow with scenting vanilla pines whispering, so many hues of green, breathtaking beauty, and sunlight dancing everywhere. His arms encircled me, and he drew me to him, holding, hugging me close. He kissed me and said he loved me. I remembered further e.e. cummings poem,

now the mountains are dancing together

How could he know so quickly? He just knew that he did as I knew I loved him.

I began calling him my Prince of Light, not knowing that in his profession he had worked with light. As I mentioned earlier, Tom was introduced to me as an optical physicist. He told me that many years ago he worked as a consultant with some of the first lasers and many other optical (light) products.

The next day, on September 1, I shared the healing method with Tom so he could let go of the fear and pain from his past experiences. At that time, Tom didn't feel that he had any to let go. He wondered: What is she talking about—"this safety stuff?" Why is she making a big deal of "I'm safe.?" (Macho me, etc.)

He had always taken care of himself and had been in many dangerous situations. He had been brave. Tom thought safety had not been a problem for him. He did want me to show him how I work with people. He does think my method has important benefits for others who have been stuck with fear and pain. I knew he was probably just not aware of his feelings of fear and pain. I led him through the work sheet and self-evaluation test I had developed to demonstrate the method. As a result, he opened and shared a painful experience in his past, and then other stories of fear and pain in his life that had not been resolved. One of his problems was that when he was 8 years old, he had an association with a happy, beautiful place at a lake with family and friends, and yet with a foreboding of loss—that it wasn't going to last. This is a symptom of a double bind.

Now the spiritual dimension is giving Tom a beautiful, happy experience and memory with family and friends of a new life and love being given to him at the Willow Lake.

Before, Tom had never really been able to deeply attach to a relationship through a home, and had spent most of his time away in a boarding school, later university and working. I realized that one of the messages he may benefit from in addition to the other messages of this method is "I am always safe living in a real home when healthy for me." How true this is for so many people who may need this message—those who have had painful experiences connected to family and home. Many people have numbed themselves, covering up their fear and pain by making choices in their lives that make them appear to feel safe. Actually, they may have been unaware that their choices were unsafe and had negative consequences. Some examples have been overworking, addictions, lack of planning and procrastination.

Returning

Dreaming one day we'd be together now
Healing our wounds before the crown
Filling the room your spirit and mine
Unveiling our souls enraptured in time
Returning with you to love we knew
Filling our hearts with grace anew
Enveloping our tender souls we entwine
Knowing quintessential bliss divine
Seeing our bond has continually grown
Flowering seeds we have truly sown
Feeling blessed peace we have at last
Understanding, Forgiving, all is past
Trusting completely our love is true
Returning we are to love we knew

(Written 1993)

Tom: The next morning, I cut more wood and then cleaned up to go for the lunch with Judy at her house. We had a pleasant lunch with another friend who had to leave early. I drove my friend back to my brother's house, and then returned to be with Judy again. In spirit, we haven't been apart since. After helping her work on a letter of importance, she offered to take me for a hike to see her wonderful meadow.

We had already shared in the delights of the mystical willow pond, and had walked around the nearby upper meadow with its special giant apple tree. She had said it was her son's favorite apple tree (a banana apple). He had discovered the tree years before while exploring around here. She wanted to share another special beautiful meadow on her side of the forest. As we walked, Judy shared a number of spiritual experiences that had happened in her life.

As we hiked, the trail wound around, and suddenly we walked through lush over-hanging trees—a portal to the grand opening into her special meadow. I felt so moved that I reached to hug her. I kissed her and she responded. It was magical. I surprised myself when I told her I loved her—just natural, my heart was full. I felt what I said, and this was very unusual for me to express any close personal feelings so quickly. As we got to know each other, we felt we are soul mates.

While walking back to the house, I saw what I thought was mistletoe over the path, and I wanted to kiss her again. I took a piece of it, held it over her head and said, "from missiles to mistletoe." (Unknown to Judy, just weeks before, I had finished a consulting job on how to use very faint satellite radio signals to guide a Navy anti-radar missile.) Our love took off like a rocket. She is my soul mate—I am blessed!

Healing Treasures

Hidden evening treasures
    amidst starring twilight sky
Twinkling multitudes of diamonds,
    seeing beyond your soulful eyes

Love's sweet ecstasy illuminating
    horizons iridescent forevermore
Now gracefully dancing, opening clouds,
    glistening celestial doors

My heart holding secret of secrets
    caring Spirit only knew
Revealing echoing spheres
    unveiling softly "I've always loved you"

Deciphered messages compelling
    Universal Grace, Love and Peace
Realizing it was never, ever you
    causing fear and pain within me

No longer hurting ourselves or others,
    through illusions clearly we see
In Grace always safety unlocking happy souls,
    our eternal golden key

Valuing precious gift of Life you give,
    simply because we breathe
Releasing death, death releasing we,
    forever paradise, we are free

From ignorance, embracing compassion,
    blind and deaf we come from to be
Caring, leading gently others, whispering green
    forests because bountiful trees

Remember healing treasures, loving, being loved,
glistening sacred dew
So good, it is true my joyous soul, my Life
because of always loving you.

(Written 1993)

[41]   Leighton, Margaret, *Shelley's Mary, The Life of Mary Godwin Shelley*, (New York, Farrar, Straus and Giroux, 1973).

[42] Leighton, Margaret, *Judith of France*, (Boston, Houghton Mifflin Co., The Riverside Press Cambridge, 1948).

[43]   E.E. Cummings: The Complete Poems 1904-1962, edited by George Firmage, (New York, Liveright Publishing Co., 1991).

RENASCENCE
(Stanza)

Through which my shrinking sight did pass
Whispered to me a word whose sound
Deafened the air for worlds around
And brought unmuffled to my ears
The gossiping of friendly spheres,
The creaking of the tented sky,
Immensity made manifold;
The ticking of Eternity

by Edna St. Vincent Millay (1892-1950)
(order slightly altered)

12. The Birthday Gift

J UDY: THE NEXT WEEKEND was my birthday, and I knew Tom was my birthday gift. Tom arrived on Wednesday, and on Thursday I read him all the poetry I had written over the years for my future soul mate. Tears came to his eyes as I read each one.

Over the weekend of my birthday, on one of our afternoons together, I wanted to read him one of my favorite poems by Edna St. Vincent Millay called "Renascence."[44]

Even though this is one of my favorite poems, I hadn't read the whole poem in a long time. Even more amazing was that I did not remember the part about a storm.

One of the sections of her very long beautiful poem has always reminded me of my own experiences of presenting this healing method to so many people.

I rarely had read through the following section, and didn't remember a storm or cry for new birth, and this was my birthday—a beautiful sunny day. I began reading out loud, and by the 4th page, unexpectedly, very quickly real thunderstorm clouds moved in, and nature joined with me as I read:

> "O God, I cried, give me new birth,
> And put me back upon the earth!
> Upset each cloud's gigantic gourd
> And let the heavy rain, down-poured
>
> (the heavens opened and poured torrents of rain
> down on my metal roof top)
>
> In one big torrent, set me free,
> Washing my grave away from me!
> I ceased; and through the breathless hush
> That answered me, the far-off rush

Of herald wings came whispering
Like music down the vibrant string
Of my ascending prayer, and—crash!

(Outside, thunder began to speak and came crashing
so loudly Tom could hardly hear me.)

Before the wild wind's whistling lash

(winds were dancing wildly, blowing in this fast moving storm)

The startled storm-clouds reared on high

Because of the sounds of the rain pouring on my metal roof,
and the thunder were so noisy, I wanted to stop reading. It was
difficult to even hear myself read. I stopped for a moment,
thinking I might wait until later to finish reading the poem
after the storm had passed. The experience was so powerful I
had tears in my eyes, and Tom, said, "read on."

And plunged in terror down the sky!
And the big rain in one black wave
Fell from the sky and struck my grave.

(at just that moment, lightning actually struck right outside,
close to my living room window!)

I know not how such things can be;
I only know there came to me
A fragrance such as never clings
To aught save happy living things;"

The dramatic storm-front immediately moved on, and now
for a few moments there was only the soft gentle pattering
rain—tears of joy from heaven, and then the blue skies and
sunshine appeared—all was peaceful again. Tom asked me,

"How did you do that—know to read this poem just at this time when a storm—rain, thunder and lightning was to come and match the exact moments in the poem?" I said, "I don't know. Sometimes, God creates amazing performances. The storm moved in and out on cue as though obeying a conductor through the lines of the poem." This is the most exciting birthday I've ever known!

During that weekend, Tom and I walked back to the Willow Lake to celebrate where we first met. I told Tom that last April I had been preparing to sing in an Earth Day concert. I wanted to change some of the verbs in the lyrics of some of the songs I had chosen to sing. Some of the songs, although beautiful, had messages that were expressed with verbs in the future tense which may cause weakness or a delay in achieving a desired goal. I had received permission from one composer to change the verbs in his lyrics from future to present tense, as long as I said in public what I was doing. Sometimes a tense shift gives immediacy and more incentive (energy) towards a visualized goal.

As Tom and I walked, I sang him my songs and taught them to him. He said I reminded him of the wise woman who had made the first singing magic, and the wise cat in Rudyard Kipling's *Just So Stories*[45] called "The Cat Who Walked By Himself"—(like my cat). I wasn't familiar with the story, and Tom began to recite some of the story for me.

Tom: Judy had given me her manuscript draft to take back to the city with me. During the week I had time to read further. I found it interesting that my unique and varied technical background had prepared me to understand her discoveries and work. My background includes: design of aerial reconnaissance cameras, infra-red scanners, radar mappers, electronic countermeasures, laser systems, image processing, pattern recognition, radio communications, intelligence data information storage/retrieval, and holography. My interest in all of these was led by my wish to aid in preventing war and creating peace.

My background in physics and engineering systems and work as a consultant and trouble-shooter for many different companies in various fields had made it possible for me to see and understand the interwoven problems she was addressing. Those problems included double binds (conflicts in language and logic contributing to mental/emotional traps). I was interested in her discoveries of causes, some solutions, and how they worked on the whole psyche of a person through the healing method itself. Through her manuscript draft, I was able to see the interconnected systems in the physiology and psychology of the body, mind and emotions. Her use of the language of physics as a metaphor to explain some phenomena in her method is apt.

There is even an interesting connection between Judy, the astronauts she mentioned in Chapter 1, and me. The astronaut's first Mercury space capsule was a version of the payload capsule of the secret large camera system we had developed a few years earlier to photograph the Soviet Bloc from satellites. I was working on that design in 1960, when the old U-2 spy plane—(another secret recce-project on which I had been system-optical-engineer) was finally shot down after a half-decade of operation.

The following week we celebrated her birthday, and she said I was her birthday gift. We were in love, and I drove up every weekend to see her. The next week she read to me out of my mother's book, *Judith of France*, which I realized I hadn't completely read before. We read further.

After the King of England, Judith's husband, dies, she found herself trapped in a web of family jealousies and other complications that put her life in great danger. The priest, John Scotus, sent the ablest knight Baudoin Bras de Fer to rescue her and bring her back to France. By escaping England, she achieved her mission to never cause strife for the family and England. Judith eventually married the knight Baudoin Bras de Fer, and they became the Count and Countess of Flanders.

Judy: We began calling each other every day, and Tom drove in from the ocean to see me every weekend. The following week, on Sunday, I was looking for a reference to Judith of France in one of my history books. She was not mentioned. I did find a Judith who had married someone named Tostig. When I looked her up, Tom and I were amazed to see she was married to a son of a Godwin, the Earl Godwin, (my family name) governor of Wessex. This was another unexpected coincidence.

This Judith was the daughter of the Count of Flanders. This was approximately 1050 A.D. Was this Judith related to the Judith of France who married again and became the Countess of Flanders in approximately 856 A.D.? Also, Godwin's nephew Sweyn became ruler of Denmark. In my own family, one of my relatives, a Godwin, married a woman of Danish descent. When I was 10 years old, we visited her relatives in Denmark. I was just looking for a reference to Judith of France and was mysteriously led to a Judith married to a Tostig Godwin. What could all this mean!? We both were intrigued!

Then we were reviewing the write-up of my adventures of being led to Historic Lambeth Palace where I gave my paper on some ideas to aid in freeing and returning safely Terry Waite and other hostages. Tom suddenly remarked: An ancestor of his had a most unusual and close connection with Lambeth Palace and the Archbishop of Canterbury three and a half centuries ago.

In parallel to me, this relative, Dr. Alexander Leighton, (1568-1649), a medical doctor, also worked with the healing of people and, like me, he wrote about freeing people from the effects of flaws in their interpretations of some religious doctrine.

Tom: This ancestor from Scotland, Dr. Alexander Leighton is known in English history as an early martyr for "Freedom of the Press," in the time of the ill-advised and ill-fated King Charles I. I just now realized the parallel coincidence that what he wrote also led him, too, into Lambeth Palace, like Judy, but in a dramatically different way. There was little grace involved for him.

Alexander Leighton, M.D. was originally trained as a church minister at St. Andrews University in Scotland, but later studied medicine in Holland. There he met and knew most of the leaders of the English Puritans who for religious freedom, were in exile there before they sailed on the "Mayflower" to settle in America in 1620. He then practiced medicine in Southern England, but also conducted services and participated in the intense religious and political discussions of the time.

In 1625, the new King Charles I with his Aides and appointed Bishops believed in "The Divine right of Kings" to override people's rights and exert absolutist powers in all religious and civil matters. By 1628 the struggle with Parliament that eventually led to the English civil war was heating up. (It was the time of the English "Petition of Right" the predecessor of our own "Bill of Rights" one and a half centuries later.)

The King's main government official was William Laud, who was also the Bishop of London. Dr. Leighton wrote a book called *An Appeal to Parliament: Sion's Plea Against the Prelacie*[46] which was a protest against Laud's moves to increase the excessive powers of the Bishops over political as well as religious matters—usurping people's old rights.

Leighton recommended the Bishops' powers should be strongly cut back.

Bishop Laud then instigated the infamous Star-Chamber proceedings to have Leighton imprisoned, and suppressed his book. In a series of closed Star-Chamber trials and interrogations, Leighton, despite repeated torture, refused to implicate others who had helped distribute the book and cogently argued against the illegal proceedings. Bishop Laud and his Star Chamber court had him publicly whipped, maimed and imprisoned for life.

Parliament was sent home. For almost a dozen years while Dr. Leighton languished in prison, the King (and Laud) ruled without Parliament. Bishop Laud was promoted to Archbishop of Canterbury and moved into Lambeth Palace, meanwhile sending more protestors to mutilation and prison—some accused as "followers of Dr.Leighton," who kept up contact with friends of freedom outside.

Eventually in 1640, the King so needed money that at last he called a new Parliament, which immediately insisted that the King release Leighton and some others from prison. They made Archbishop Laud pay "the good doctor" 10,000 pounds in damages for Laud's illegal use of the Star Chamber Court against him. Within a month, Parliament had impeached Laud and another government minister, the Earl of Stafford. The self-centered King, needing Parliament (for now) more than his favorite Councilors, threw them in the Tower, and in a few months even signed Stafford's death-warrant.

However, in a year the English Civil War was intermittently underway. After a Royalist uprising, Lambeth Palace was confiscated and turned into a prison to hold Royalist officers. Parliament then pointedly named Dr. Leighton to be its nominal Warden—in command of Lambeth Palace with his former persecutor the Archbishop of Canterbury Laud as his star boarder.

Despite the ironic turnabout, Leighton never retaliated against his prisoner and former persecutor; instead showing him grace and compassion. Laud's only complaint was that Dr. Leighton made him pay extra to allow his servants to come serve him in his own palace.

Laud was eventually executed for his other crimes in 1645, and the tyrant King Charles I followed 4 years later. Their lack of understanding true grace and compassion had only inflamed the problems and passions on all sides, which to some degree are still alive today.

After a decade with no King, the more sensible royal son was restored to the throne as King Charles II, and we note that he appointed Dr. Leighton's own son, Robert, to be Archbishop of Glasgow, where he worked to bring peace among the opposing factions after the Restoration.

Judy: For centuries various groups have worked to bring peace, and attempted to legislate peace between warring groups. For many, all this work and written peace treaties, although extremely valuable, did not resolve their hatred, their fear and pain from the past, their desire for revenge, nor give them flexibility in tolerance of differing beliefs. Their misunderstandings, pain, and wars have continued.

In *A Path To Light*, I describe how flaws in language and beliefs may have crept in over time from early civilizations. This unknowingly created mental/emotional traps (misunderstandings) that were transferred even into religions through some of their interpretations, as well as other institutions. This book, as well as *A Path to Light* describe my healing method on how to get free from many traps, acquire a healthy self-worth, let go of unnecessary fear, pain, guilt or numbness, and make many more wise healthy choices.

Throughout history, surprisingly, one of the traps causing confusion and controversy involved the misinterpretation of the concept of grace. Defining just who was eligible to receive grace and just how, were issues. These issues intermingled with other issues which caused misunderstandings even about cause and effect, which created more confusion and conflict.

Some answers are presented as to the meaning of grace, and examples of receiving and giving universal grace. Actual steps—how to be in the state of universal grace and compassion are given in Chapter 17: (Path of Discovery).

Many years ago, when I was presenting my method in a booth at a convention center, a lady came and asked me what I thought of past lives? She told me that she had experienced 100 past lives. I told her that I didn't have any memory of such an experience myself. I do think that whether reincarnation is so or not, that this life is an opportunity to learn, and do (act). The message of universal grace (forgiveness, mercy, compassion, and unmerited love) is a vital lesson to learn and live.

The next week Tom and I began writing some poetry to each other. The following was Tom's first to me:

Gladly Stay

Although I'm far away from near,
Heart's with Heart so far away
I know that You and I are We
A longing draws me near to thee
Far and nearing, nearly here
Soon to touch and gladly stay

—On September 24, Tom wrote this special poem for me:

The Willow Lake

Her Angel's wonder led me there
Far up the mystic glade.
A willowed pond (that needed care)
For somehow I was made:

To bring and plant the thousand flowers
That grace the lake—we toiled for hours—
Then laid a pipeline down the hill
with water from a tangled rill
So they could drink their fill.

Yet all the while still unaware
That she, from time to time was there
to note with pleasure what we wrought—
A place for contemplative thought—
yet one you need to share!

By mystic helpers, I surmise,
(Thru synchronicity divine
And complex plan): This simple man;
This Angel, beautiful and wise;
were drawn to find this place so fair
That won her heart and mine!

For half a moon the planted seeds
Replacing all the ancient weeds
Prepared the way to see
And on a second Mystic Day
by Fate in unison to say:
"This is the one for me!"

And now we know that it is so.
We know by stars above—
We have a lifetime more to go—
We have each other's Love.

(I wrote the following poem for Tom)

A Path to Light

Heralding twilight, God whispers willow lake
    beckoning Angels "Come to me"
Inviting Timelessness, timing soul mate's
    opening heart reaching out for thee
Overflowing cup, running water meeting waters
    calling souls softly within we
Journeying down hillside gallantly, path
    flowering daffys prepared you for me
Echoing soul mate's bereaving heart, pleading
    silent tears floating among alder trees
Sparkling eyes glowing, my Prince of Light,
    drawing I to you, releasing my heart free

Laughing voices, immersing yesterdays, birthing
    present, searching our loving bond
Climbing stairs, lighting path to Light, gloriously
    watching, twinkling memories fond
Dining lights flickering midst mystic moments
    dauntlessly circling melodies' air
Walking home, sharing shyly hands pulsing, uneven
    ground protecting us with care
Leaving your flashlight, taking my Sunshine
    illuminating your soulful path returning
Morning First Light leading me floating back
    bringing you hidden secrets of healing

Departing, took flight winking City of Lights
    finding Mother's books enlightening
Reading *Judith of France* unveiling life's mission
    delivering grace and mercy all giving
Rejoicing my heart imploring yours to impart
    awaiting our divine second meeting
Evening family dinner, shining stars sparkling
    every thought, electrifying feelings

Becoming tomorrow's every today wandering
   magical meadow glistening
Looking to your eyes mesmerizing your capturing
   arms surrounding me beaming
Kissing First Light blazing golden waves radiating
   passions reverberating, souls perfecting
Whispering you, I love you, oscillating tidal waves,
   surrendering wholeness, ours sanctifying

Walk with I, you want with me knowing lofty way
   joyfully, glowing too
Souls enrapturing, bliss flowering, flowing from dew
   to morning dew
Silently reach me prayer writing before today
   drawing sweetly you to I
Together now spiriting we to one beyond bright
   crystal lining sunlit skies
Jubilant tears, finding you here, knowing
   incomplete, wanting missing years
Poetic rhymes, chiming minds, singing eternal
   truth, bridging golden spheres

Sharing First Light to rapturing First Light
   increasing kindly our dawning insights
Liberating suffering lessons teaching, flashes
   recognizing eyes leading to reunite
Scintillating trail, our footsteps traveling, timing
   your closer harmony embracing me
Approaching, longing, loving paths joining,
   culminating our highest calling within we
Lighting way reaching together pristine distant
   pasts revealing love gently grown
Crystallizing memories, endearing seconds,
   wayfaring forested mountains our own

Reflecting stars, gems dancing earth, deer childly
prancing meadows, First Light melting dew
Timing every First Light wrapping silken mornings
joyful reminiscing always I be with you
Voyaging land blossoming forget-me-nots traveling
sanctuary we trust unknowing
Meandering shimmering meadows, virgining
forget-me-nots calling, love all showing
Waving thistle puffs, lavender hues, spinning
spiders filigree, graciously we bend
Discovering yarrow lacing delicately revealing
life's warm secrets floating the wind
Misting springs, streams, lakes, tears, endlessly
gratitude, ever showering from my heart
Remembering destiny repeating, azure eyes blue,
yours awakening my soul from the start

[44]   Millay, Edna St. Vincent, *Renascence and Other Poems*, (New York: Mitchell Kennerly, 1917).

[45]   Kipling Rudyard, *Just So Stories*, (New York, Penguin Books, USA, Inc., 1974).

[46]   Leighton, Alexander, MD, *An Appeal to Parliament: Sion's Plea Against the Prelacie*, (Holland, 1628)

13. WE ARE THE TREASURE SAFE TO KEEP

You Stay

Music drifting loftily lilting, prayers searching
    and You stay
Breezes blowing warmly freeing, tousling
    tresses and You want to stay
Clouds playing images drifting beyond, feathering
    and You stay
Sun soothing warmth comforting hearts caring
    and You vow to stay
Moon bringing rest becalming til dawning
    and You joyfully stay
All these passing, more passing away,
    and You lovingly stay

(Written 1976)

THE WEEKEND BEFORE WE got married, we spent completing the reading of one of Tom's mother's books, *The Secret of the Old House.*[47] This book is autobiographical of their family when they lived in Virginia the year Tom was eight years old. Tom thought he had read it years ago. It was published when Tom was 15 years old. As we took turns reading to each other, and the story kept unfolding, he realized he had never completed the book. I was concerned when we reached the part of the story where the children were noticing their mother and father were very worried. I didn't think that Tom's mother would have been writing about the time when her husband was very ill, and then eventually passed away. I

155

wasn't sure, and took some deep breaths. Continuing to read on, we discovered they were worried about another serious problem. Also, David, who represented Tom in his mother's books, had found an unusual rock that becomes his secret amulet. This reminded me of when I found the special crystal rock in the shape of a heart on the land where I lived. Time will tell whether Tom is led to a treasure. On Sunday evening we completed reading her book.

Then, I shared two letters from my past. One letter was from my first real boyfriend when I was a senior in high school, and the other from a person I met in Hawaii the year before I was to move to Los Angeles. Even though they were both kind, good people, I thought and felt I had to walk away from them in order to meet my destiny, whatever that was.

My friend in Hawaii flew with me when I was moving to Los Angeles in June 1979. A few hours later he was flying to do business in France. I had explained to him that I didn't think it was best for either of us to have a long distance relationship. He knew that I was moving to Los Angeles to train with a master concert pianist. The next month he sent me a letter and a poem in French. He had missed his connecting train in Paris at 1:00 a.m. and no hotel. After visiting the coffee shops and bars until they closed at 4:00 a.m., he had dozed in a park. The last coffee shop he tried was called the Maison du Poets which was closed. There was a poem on the closed door. This was the poem he sent me. The last and only time he came to see me in Los Angeles was in the summer because I knew that continuing our relationship was not best for both of us. He was offered a new position in a university in another state. In life's spiritual timing we both eventually married someone else.

Not only had I never asked him to translate the poem for me, I had never shown his letter to anyone or asked anyone to translate the poem. I had one year of French in college and didn't bother to learn more to translate it myself. For almost 19 years this poem had been hidden and undeciphered.

Here I was showing this poem to Tom the day before we are to be married, and asking him to translate it for me as he knows some French. There was no title on the page, although recently I found the title to be *Le Jardin* (French), *The Garden* (English). The following are two lines from the poem that Tom translated:

The sweet moment of eternity
Where we embraced[48]

That door had been closed, and now opened with Tom translating it for me. I shared this with Tom so he could see and feel in greater depth my search for him that had been so focused. I walked away from others when I discovered more clues that they were not the one for me. Sometimes I was misled in the beginning. The older, wiser, and more experienced I became, the better able I was to know what clues to look for to make wiser choices. Sometimes though, I wondered whether I was engaged in just wishful thinking, and wondered what spiritual adventure God and the angels would lead me on next. We were so excited looking forward to our wedding ceremony the next day.

On our way to our wedding, I shared with Tom that maybe his mother's gift to him and his brother and sisters in *The Secret of the Old House*[49] was by ending the story in a happy way—their finding a treasure that might save them—helping assuage her pain and healing from the loss of her husband, as well as soothing for all of them to aid in their recovery from the loss of their father. Together at last, we add to the treasures of our hearts. I reminded Tom of the last line of my poem, "Love's Prayer" for him.

"We are the treasure safe to keep."

The day was cloudy and looked like rain. I asked God and the Angels to please move the clouds around and bring the sunshine out for us, and the sun began gradually to spread its shining light.

During our ceremony, I was so moved by Tom's eyes, his voice, and emotion when he was repeating his vows to me, and my own emotions that I started to cry as I began to repeat my vows to Tom. I know that almost everyone feels very special when they are repeating their wedding vows, and for me I felt them so deeply. When we walked outside the sun was shining brilliantly, blue skies and puffy white clouds everywhere.

That evening we planned to go to dinner at a Chinese restaurant on the coast. Six months earlier, we had gone there for the first time when Tom brought me to the city to see where he lived and worked. We had such a beautiful time then, and enjoyed comparing our thoughts and feelings now with how we thought and felt then. We even sat at the same table where we sat before, and ordered the same food. When we got our fortune cookies, we had another amazing experience that brought tears to my eyes.

Mine read, "God gives you everything that you want."

Tom's read, "You are tasting the sweets of success."

We both feel extraordinarily blessed, our closeness always continuing and happiness as we both have never known until now.

---

[47]   Leighton, Margaret, *Secret of the Old House*, (Philadelphia, John C. Winston Co., 1941).

[48]   Prevert, Jacques, *Le Jardin* (French), *The Garden* (English)

[49]   Leighton, Margaret, *Secret of the Old House*, (Philadelphia, John C. Winston Co., 1941)

---

14. THANKSGIVING PRAYER ANSWERED

JUDY: IN OCTOBER 1997, Tom took me to his high school reunion at the Webb School for its 75th anniversary. We had a beautiful visit back to his past, meeting some of his high school friends.

Heavenly Walk

Walking through time sharing glorious life,
    I being with you
Hearts unexpectedly harmonizing in tune,
    opening to renew

Inspiriting good will flourishing, resplendent
    holiday evening air
As we walk exhilarated, time together,
    embracing everywhere

Circling carousel horses, you lovingly
    painted colors for me
Ferris wheel lights turning, little children
    riding the wind with glee

Floating boats amid lofty dreams, spiraling
    buoyantly in air
Returning home to loving youth with me,
    filled with gentle care

Echoing laughter shimmering leaves in trees,
    passing childhood school
Reliving our lasting fond memories,
    so kindly carrying us through

Wafting chimney fires, blossoming roses
    perfuming, celebrate festive air
Continuing our walk through eternal time,
    meaningful journeys to share

Creating timeless present, uniting sublimely
    myriad grace-filled pasts
Launching joyous memories, our tears, warm
    forever, evergreen to last

Transforming our souls, pine tree scents,
    enchanted beyond time in air
Heavenly walk, starry night, touching I to you
    majestically everywhere

(Written 1993)

In November 1997, Tom told me our relationship reminded him of the story, "The Gift of the Magi," by O. Henry.[50] The story is of a couple, very happily married who didn't have many possessions. They did posses a beautiful love that led them to sacrifice for each other.

Thanksgiving and Christmas of 1997, were warm and wonderful as we gathered at our original meeting place in the oil lamp-lit house in the mountains with relatives from both of our families.

The day after Thanksgiving we experienced another spiritual coincidence with Tom's family. They came over to our ranch house for a visit. His brother-in-law said that back in 1941, he had been here during the time the water reservoir-swimming pool was being built in front of our house by the military. Then they told us the exciting story of their first romantic meeting back in 1943, at the same old house near where we met last August. This is the house that I had wondered about, when I was searching for my cat when I had first moved in the year before—wondering whether the owner might lead me to my soul mate.

The previous Thanksgiving of November 1996, had brought me several gifts of good fortune. My daughter had introduced me to her writer friend, some months before at one of her performances. After listening to him talk about one of the scripts he was writing, I told him about my manuscript, and he asked to read it. We met the day before that Thanksgiving of 1996, and he gave me valuable editing suggestions, and chapter title of "First Light" *meaning shining light on new solutions to the problems of double binds.*

All of a sudden, I remembered that my late father had once told me that we were related to Frances Scott Key who wrote the "Star Spangled Banner." Immediately, I repeated the lines "Oh say can you see, by the dawn's early light," and I knew the title he had chosen is perfect for a section of my manuscript *A Path to Light.*

He also suggested that I write a chapter explaining the collective subconscious, which turned into two chapters—one called "Psychobiologic Binds." I had avoided putting the information in the manuscript. Even though the healing method is simple, explaining how and why it works is complex because of interwoven problems (mental/emotional traps). Now, that the major work of writing the manuscript was finished, I could totally focus on explaining how and why using the healing method may work so quickly.

Also, several weeks before that Thanksgiving, a friend told me about a job that a friend of his was leaving, and that I could apply. I was interviewed, and accepted a position as secretary to the owner of a company which owned property out in the wilderness. He wanted to move the next month to a house out there where I would work part-time as a secretary. He would only go there a few days a week to work and later only once a month. Accepting this job in such an isolated place, I thought I would have more free time to concentrate on my writing. I felt I was being given a magnificent jewel—a beautiful, peaceful and isolated place with a great expansive view to finish my book. The owner had also hired a caretaker and his wife to live in another house close by on the property so I wasn't completely alone. As far as I knew, I thought I had only one more chapter to write and then the editing.

In December, my son, along with some friends and their sons helped me to move. When my son saw where I would be living, he asked me how I had manifested such a wonderful place to live. I wasn't sure. I told God that I would like to live more "simply." There were five deer to greet us the day we moved there. Some people wondered whether something was wrong with me to move to such a remote place. I thought this was an opportunity of a lifetime to live so close to nature in such an idyllic place. Was I living in a spiritual dream? Yes, and true to life.

After the move, I settled into my new home and job in the wilderness. In January, several feet of snow fell, and I was able to cross-country ski, leaving from my backdoor. The beauty in the evenings, walking home past a lake iced over with a reflected moon, the cattails and trees all laced with snow was so inspiring. The scene looked like a winter holiday picture from a nature magazine. What a romantic place to live! I wished I had someone to share this joy and beauty.

Soon the beautiful winter wonderland evolved into blizzards, and often 90-mile-an hour icy gales. I saw why the house was built so solidly. The joy of cross-country skiing from my backdoor turned into a necessity (carrying in groceries in a backpack from where the snow plow had given up). One late evening, a neighbor snowplowed a place for my car on the road outside the property. By myself, I made my way through the deep snowdrifts passing by my moonlit lake—snow crystals transforming evergreen trees, cattails, and even dormant branches into a glistening crystal palace, all reflecting in the ice covered lake. I wished I had someone to share this. One week the snowstorms became so frequent leaving deep snow blankets that even the caretaker and his wife left for the nearby village to stay with friends. There I was alone with my two cats and dogs who needed reassurance and comfort. They would huddle around me on my bed at night, meowing and barking at the turbulent 90-mile-an hour high winds.

No one had warned me that this house was in direct line with a canyon wind-tunnel. The winds would blow day and night for weeks at a time shaking the whole house, which was made of brick. I wondered when the winds would take a breather. To comfort myself at night, I began to pretend that I was on a roller coaster rocking me to sleep. I enjoyed every moment of these unexpected nature adventures feeling totally alive.

By February, I got back my manuscript again—rearranging the order and logical flow (from the simple to the complex), and a new chapter explaining psychobiologic binds and the collective subconscious—editing along the lines my writer friend had suggested months before. My daughter had loaned me her computer while she was away. Then I became more seriously focused on how to construct the additional chapter to describe some of my new discoveries and contributions. These were to help explain just why the seemingly simple aspects of the method actually work so well.

In March 1997, I called Dr. Marcolongo, Ph.D. psychologist and relayed the mission of my manuscript. We had worked together periodically since 1987, and he understood my healing method. He had referred people to me to learn my method, and had been one of the editors for the introduction of my cassette tapes. I knew that I could trust him to be a thorough critic and advisor on editing suggestions. I asked him whether he would be interested in giving me his criticisms of my manuscript, and that I had one more chapter to write. He kindly offered to help me. Dr. Marcolongo has a wonderful library, and I began

asking for particular books I thought I would need. He found
them and more. His wife, Donna was also a great support and
assistance to me.

In June 1997, Psychiatrist Dr. Baron, my consultant, as I
mentioned before, reviewed my last chapter and suggested
I include some simple stories demonstrating some of the
"double binds" (mental/emotional traps) described by the
psychotherapist, Paul Watzlawick, et al.[51] I created stories to
demonstrate the steps that had been set up, describing the
double bind. By the second week in July this new version of
the manuscript was ready to send to an agent.

Memories of gratitude float through my mind thinking
of the many past years working with Dr. Baron and Dr.
Marcolongo. Several cancer patients had asked me to create
an introduction for my relaxation tapes, briefly explaining the
major points of my method to help them remember. (Many
people with chronic stress, depression and/or chronic diseases
have to take care of so much.) I recall after Dr. Marcolongo
assisted me with the editing of the introduction to my cassette
tape—I got on the elevator with my arms full of the edited
papers. An older couple was on the elevator. The man said
to me, "That looks like the Declaration of Independence!"
I asked, "How did you know?" His wife said, "He's blind."
I replied, "He sees more than you think he sees. This is the
Declaration of Independence for the human soul." Also,
around this time someone said to me, "Do you realize that
what you discovered may turn the world *upside down?*" This
was in 1989.

After I met with Dr. Baron at the NIMH, where he worked
with me on the final editing of this brief introductory summary
of the method, I was ready to record my cassette tapes.

Several years later in 1991, a humorous incident happened.
I ordered new labels to be printed for my 30-minute cassette
tapes. When I picked up the labels, they had been printed
upside-down. The manager had a worried look on his face,
but I remembered back to two years earlier when a person

had laughingly said, "your method may turn the world upside-down!" I told the manager that the labels were just fine upside-down and shared the story with him. We had a joyful laugh at the fulfillment of a fortuitous sign. At that time, I no idea that my *own life* would seem to turn upside down to place me on the path to eventually meet my soul mate.

My mind travels back to the time in January 1993, when I went to the Philadelphia area to work with Dr. Baron, who was then President and Medical Director of an acute-care psychiatric hospital (meaning in-patients could only stay for two weeks). My friend, Joan was so kind to have me stay with her and her family, and drove me quite some distance, back and forth to the hospital the days I was there. Dr. Baron and I were to work together on writing a research grant application on using my healing method with cancer patients for the Office of Alternative Medicine.

Dr. Baron asked me to explain my healing method to a group of medical students, and to demonstrate it with two in-patients who had recently attempted suicide. In explaining my healing method, I illustrated a particular double bind (a mental/emotional trap) related to punishment, fear and pain, and self-worth. In 1985, I had discovered a painful maze of interwoven conflicts in myself, and developed a method for resolving them.

Many of the people (children and adults), I was a consultant for, had revealed a similar pattern through my work sheets. In addition to other problems, including fear, pain, and guilt from the past (*unforgiven experiences, and those forgiven but with still unresolved pain*), they were also suffering with guilt associated with God—they thought they were being punished by God, themselves and others. Because of misunderstanding and misinterpretations, they gave inaccurate reasons about who was punishing them, and why. To add to their confusion, many felt they must have been bad people, and didn't deserve to feel happy or receive Grace (internalize compassion, forgiveness and unmerited love.) They also didn't know how to transition to a non-punishment state. This included even those who had done confessions and penance. Also, many people, who didn't believe in God, had been unable to stop punishing themselves or others (i.e., also had been unable to forgive).

Because of misunderstood interpretations of words and ideas, many people have either not wanted to deal with this controversial tangled topic or did not know how. It is easy to understand why many people, in their former therapies, hadn't stopped punishing themselves or others. For some, their view that God was punishing them, and their lack of knowledge about how to stop their punishment created other interwoven problems and traps.

When people have felt punished, many times they were unable to forgive themselves and others, and let go of pain. Additionally, they also may have had subconscious guilt about acquiring knowledge and wisdom. This made it difficult to figure out how to stop the unnecessary fear and pain, and have a healthy self-worth. This became a locked-in circle pattern (interwoven loop) of fear and pain. (Many people thought that they had to be perfect in order to be 100% valuable. Sometimes they didn't know enough to prevent or solve a problem, yet had been afraid to find out, know enough, or be a know-it-all, a mental/emotional trap.) Also, they didn't know that, *"I'm 100% valuable, even when I may not know how to prevent or solve a problem."*

The late Abraham Maslow, Ph.D. psychologist, also described some problems in acquiring knowledge in his chapter "The Need to Know and the Fear of Knowing" as follows:

> All those psychological and social factors that increase fear will cut our impulse to know; all factors that permit courage, freedom and boldness will thereby also free our need to know.[52]

In order to untangle the tangle related to learning and knowing, I created the message: *"I am always safe living and being wise when healthy for me."* This works together with the other messages of the healing method giving you a positive connection bridging between your healthy self-worth and the ideas *of being safe to live, learn, know and be wise.* (Wisdom also includes learning and knowing when and how you can safely tell what you know.) Also an aid in solving the trap is to focus on and accept *"I am always safe, valuable and cared for because I have the gift of life," (even when I don't know it all.)* Your evidence for this is that you are here, and you *have* received *some* opportunities and blessings. These problems and solutions are discussed in greater detail in my book, *A Path to Light.*

For me, one of the steps in healing was to recognize that grace is a **universal principle.** Grace means mercy, compassion, forgiveness, and unmerited love. By focusing on the above messages, I began a process which assisted me to further understand how I am "safely releasing" myself from *unnecessary fear and pain.* This was a key to freeing myself from the habit and fear of that *fear and pain.* This is important, because many have also been using fear and pain as a form (an illusion) of protective defense. With diminishing anxiety and clutter, you may have greater clarity, see more to see how to free yourself from mental/emotional traps. Further clarity about how, may happen as you fill in the Self-worth Exercise on pp. 236-241.

After I spoke with the medical students, I went on to demonstrate the method with two of the in-patients in the hospital. Both of them had each very recently attempted suicide. I consulted individually for them on **two consecutive days.** In addition to their many problems, they both had the added problem of thinking God was punishing them. Their reaction to the healing method was immediate and dramatic. By the end of our **first session,** very quickly through the method, they each had released themselves from their immediate despair of the darkness and pain in themselves. With the use of my method, they put themselves on a path of light in grace and compassion for themselves and others.

The next morning, during Dr. Baron's rounds, each of the patients enthusiastically asked to work with me again, which I did. In only two sessions, they received immediate relief, and thereafter continued using my cassette tape and work sheet as self-support to aid themselves in further identifying and releasing mental/emotional traps. Because of my consulting for people back in Los Angeles, I wasn't able to stay longer. Three years later in 1996, Dr. Baron said that one of the people called and asked for my phone number to get another cassette tape. She had misplaced my tape during a recent move. She said that my method and cassette tape were some of the tools that had been a great benefit to her, and continues to use them.

Because of consulting for people in an emergency, high-stress state, or who are very busy, I created a simple tool to use. This consists of two-pages with the healing steps to my method found in the Appendix: Preventive and Healing Kit. The messages can be quickly memorized and repeated during a short break. This can be done a number of times throughout the day, and before falling asleep in a matter of a few minutes. (I slowly repeated each message 4 times.)

There have been concerns about unconditional love and compassion that have been expressed by some others, including Dr. Abraham Maslow. He said the following:

> Unless capacity for Compassion through under-standing is supplemented by the capacity for anger, disapproval and indignation, the result may be a flattening of all affect, a blandness, in reaction to people, inability to be indignant and a loss of discrimination of and taste for real capacity, skill, superiority and excellence.
>
> B-cognition (unconditional love, compassion) can lead to undiscriminating acceptance, to blurring

of everyday values, to loss of taste, to too great a tolerance.[53]

Focusing on the following message aids in solving this problem, which is added to all the other messages of this method:

"I am always safe not blaming
or judging when healthy for me."

This translates that there *is* wise and *healthy blaming and judging* (knowing cause and effect, and having the ability to come to opinions of things; power of comparing and deciding; understanding; good sense) without degrading myself and others. I remain compassionate for myself and others, understanding and remembering the human dilemma of all people having learned misinformation. This has created confusion and mental/emotional traps that have caused many people to not have the tools to live with dignity and respect for themselves or others. With an attitude of grace, compassion and dignity for all, I am able to feel when I am uncomfortable, understand, make a judgment, and walk away from unnecessary painful situations. Many times I can see when, and often why others can't see or understand.

When children are young and not getting along with each other, a truce can be called, separate them, and tell them that when they figure out how to get along, they can be together again. Very quickly they may resolve their differences, and be happily playing again. Since we can do this, surely God can do no less.

Many people have suffered the consequences of their destructive behavior, and still were unable to change. With a kind, compassionate attitude, you may be able to guide children and yourself with the tools of this healing method to *learn missing or hidden messages*. By focusing on, "I'm always safe not hurting myself or others when healthy for me," makes it easier to see probable consequences—and choose wise, constructive behavior. *Then knowing the consequences may make a difference, and* you can then offer constructive choices. When this is done, you and others may have greater clarity, to see, choose and use wise logical reasoning to resolve problems, change and heal more quickly. I also ask for God's guidance.

When teaching and studying piano, I have noticed that my students and I learn faster and enjoy ourselves without punishment. Many other people have told me they had stopped studying piano when they were young because sometimes their teachers hit their hands, yelled at them and/ or were indignant about their mistakes.

Another trap some people experience is guilt associated with making love. Some have separated the spiritual and physical sides of themselves. This may have shown itself when they felt spiritual and thought that they couldn't make love, or when they made love, in addition to not feeling spiritual, they felt unworthy. Joining your spirituality with making love with your spouse is adding wholeness, oneness, and beauty to your relationship deepening your spiritual connection with each other. In addition to the other aspects of the healing method, focusing on either of the following thoughts may be helpful . . .

"I am one with God and one with you," or
"I am one with the universe and one with you," . . .

before, during and after making love. This may replace the negative messages formerly learned which may eventually disappear.

Now, back in my new world, the day after Thanksgiving 1997, sitting under a whistling vanilla pine tree wafting vanilla fragrances through the air in our mystical meadow with sun stars dancing across the leaves, I reread Tom the following poem "Divine Light" that I had written back in 1994, about the future that is also meant for him:

Divine Light

Falling sounds, christening raindrops bringing
    me here, returning again to you
Falling sounds, ascending love, unveiling
    distant pasts evolving within we two
Falling sounds, whispering voice, comforting
    from glittering heavenly spheres
Falling sounds, loving grace, faith unfettering
    all our saddening worldly fears

Remembering long forgotten evensongs, glowing
    serenely, touching we unfold
Departing joyful hearts brought tears transpiring
    our blissful story years untold
Glimpsing pain invisibly you concealed, living
    sorrow remembering time reveals
Reaching through your pain my tears entreating,
    releasing all ancestral fears

Holding music's secret lace lilting, bonding
    together through eternal time
Crossing bridge of compassion, life fulfilling,
    lingering pastoral rhyme
Awakening again, shining sharing night, entrancing
    enlivening ecstasy to love
Morning star, gracing one and all, loving
    simply as day lighting cooing doves

Gaining all, your Life came to me, lifting
    gently, higher through the air
Filling Life, presence of you, deepening
    unaware growing feelings of care
Circling melodies, mornings surrounding
    sunshine cuddling, caressing we

Walking together kindness and we, flowering
  playful trees, breezing, swaying free

Climbing hillsides sharing time,
  lightening tale twilighting galaxies mid-air
Journeying top of world with you, glowing
  moon full, inspiring boundless we share
Passing pulsing stream of Life, twinkling
  laughter clustering, being we are whole
Moving on in timelessness, giving your hand
  to mine, candle lighting we one soul

Reaching summit octagonal, finding mystery
  reflecting joyous we beyond all
Kissing, zenith dimensions we soar, culminating
  responding our destiny call
Returning aware precious gift, Love we share,
  hugging warmly our embracing souls
Floating flowers fragrance, scenting softly, lulling
  early springtime zephyr, we roam

Patterning silhouettes canopied trees, kindling
  memories enthroning starry night
Beaming Sylvan moon hearts brim, showering
  blessings, radiating divine light
Enlightening universal grace, enjoining paths
  loving, completing cycle of birth
Thanksgiving answered prayer, lying lion with
  lamb, receiving grace on earth.

(Written 1994)

Lofty Surprise

Judy: In early December, 1997, I drove back to the mountains by myself and stayed overnight to deliver the last cat back to the owner's secretary the next day. The cat had run away the previous Monday when we took the dog and other cat to the owner.

The stresses began in the early morning. After carefully planning how to prevent the cat from running away again, in the early morning, the owner of the property came into my house to talk with me. This was okay until a workman drove up and the owner went out the door without thinking and left it open. The cat ran out and away. She had a habit of staying out for quite awhile to hunt in the forest, so I called the secretary leaving a message that I couldn't bring the cat. Then I went out to my car, opened all the doors hoping she would come back and want to investigate my car. Fortunately, about fifteen minutes later I went back outside, and she had climbed into my car.

Then there was a problem of meeting my appointment with a doctor in one town and driving to another town to meet the secretary to deliver the cat in a particular window of time. Her children were in a Christmas play that morning, and she also had other engagements to meet. She was under a lot of stress so I quickly explained my healing method, and gave her some phrases to focus on. She told me that she had been trying to remember a prayer that another author had suggested in her book, but she was under so much stress she couldn't remember the prayer. She was grateful to have a few simple phrases to bring her to peace again.

Naively, I put the cat in a box I had carefully designed for her to sit next to me so she would feel comfortable and not afraid. I could still pet some parts of her head. We drove down the mountain, wondering whether we would arrive where we were supposed to be at the right time, and reach her new home in time. She was calm and happy while I petted her. A few blocks from the doctor's office she was no longer content, and began trying to convince me that she would be just fine out of that box by chewing the hole wider. She leaped out and was happy for the rest of the trip. Even though I was later than we had planned, when I delivered the cat, the secretary was in wonderful spirits. The phrases I had given her earlier had helped her to enjoy her morning at her children's Christmas play. She was also able to adjust and could meet her luncheon date on time.

After I stopped for lunch, and as I got back into my car, the heavens opened and began to pour. I was driving on the freeway and having a very difficult time seeing. The rain was so heavy that I couldn't see well enough to change lanes and get off the road. I began to ask God to help me as I didn't want Tom to be afraid for my safety. I wanted to be safe for him so he wouldn't have to experience a loss of my love. I finally drove into the apartment area and pulled into our garage, relieved. I thought that I would call Tom and then go to sleep because I was very tired from the stresses of the whole day.

I got out of my car, and Tom came into the garage to meet me. He had been so worried when the unexpected storm blew in and was so violent. He wished he had driven with me. We both had decided that it was best for him to stay at work while I went and made the cat return, not knowing that an El Nino storm was coming. Because he was so worried, he finally left work to see whether I had returned home or left a message on our answering machine. We were both so grateful and exhilarated to see each other that we both cried. His leaving work to be there for me,' and our being safely together again was our grand Christmas present.

Miracle Magi

In early December 1997, I had been trying to remember the author and title of the story, "The Gift of the Magi" but without success. I wanted to buy the book for Tom for a Christmas gift. A week later, I was out driving looking for a dry cleaning shop.

Entering the busy parking lot of a very large modern shopping center, I tried to spot the shop among the many stores.

Then I drove to the end of the shopping center to look there, and still there was no dry cleaning shop. As I continued on to behind the shopping center where I planned to turn around, I looked up and noticed a large wood carving of a blue whale with a sign on it that said "BOOKS." This was on the side of a small one-story wooden framed house. It seemed to be held in a secret time-warp in the midst of the back parking lot, and had refused to be destroyed when the modern shopping center was built. A charming used-book store in an old two-room wooden house overflowing with books (even on the front porch) was hidden in this modern shopping center—an unlikely place.

I felt transported into a wonderland of old books and another dimension in time. In front of me at eye level, as I walked through the open door, were two volumes of the complete stories by O. Henry. Quietly appearing before me was a grandmotherly lady in charge of the shop offering to help me. I still didn't remember the author's name or the title of the story. I described the story to the lady, and she remembered the title, The Gift of the Magi, but she was not sure whether O. Henry was the author.

We began excitedly looking through the table of contents. There we found the story. I felt I had found a sparkling treasure, and later events revealed that it was true. I bought the books and hid them 'till Christmas. This quaint bookstore house seemed to have a life of its own, so I was compelled to ask about it's history. The kind lady laughed and told me that the house was born a half-century ago. It had been moved and used as an office in several different locations close by, including the shopping center where it was used by the property manager and later transformed into a bookstore. She thought that the old house was inhabited by friendly spirits. Certainly I was led there in an unusual unexpected manner.

A few hours later, Tom and I were driving to the mountains for the weekend. With tears in his eyes, he told me that in the early morning he had been looking out of the window watching the sunrise thinking of the story, "The Gift of the Magi. Again he was reminded of our living in a little apartment, not having many things, yet filled with love. Tears came to my eyes because just an hour earlier I had been in the bookshop where I was led to the books with that story by O. Henry. I told Tom I couldn't tell him yet, but that something very mystical had happened earlier in the day.

On Christmas Eve day I told Tom that Christmas Eve was going to be very special. That evening I gave him the books to open, and told him the story of our spiritual coincidence—being led to the books the same morning that he had remembered the Gift of the Magi while he was watching the sunrise. He hadn't told me about this experience until we were in the car driving. Christmas day and evening were beautiful as we celebrated being together with our families.

50 Henry, O., *The Complete Short Stories*, (Doubleday & Company, Inc., 1953), Vol. I.

51 Bateson, Gregory, and Jackson, Don D.; Haley, Jay; and Weakland, John, "Toward a Theory of Schizophrenia." *Behavior Science*, 1956, 1:251-64.

52 Maslow, Abraham H., Ph.D., *Toward A Psychology Of Being*, (New York, Van Nostrand Reinhold Company, Inc., 1968), p. 67.

53 Maslow, Abraham, *Toward A Psychology of Being*, (New Jersey, Van Nostrand, Princeton, 1968), pp. 121-122.

15. TWINKLING MEMORIES

Path of Bliss

Many lofty paths not chosen, unwinding,
    leading secretly your tenderness to me
Enfolding arms around us, purifying,
    healing completely our hearts finally free

Our hearts pulse in rhythm, encircling,
    caressing our winging infinite souls
Carrying us away, blessing, infinity enriching,
    lost, we are being whole

Laughter, chiming bells, jingling,
    flickering candlelight celebrating solstice season
Being together now, growing, knowing
    quintessence of life's 'boundaryless' reasons

Our first kiss softly, flowing, trembling,
    I'll always remember golden hues
Evening among trees, scintillating,
    inspiring loving devotion for me and you

Allay pain of world, protecting,
    cherishing kindly we generously partake
Following blissful path, reflecting eyes sparkling,
    sunlit crystal Winter snowflakes

Our gentle spirits, holding, comforting,
    turning splendorous night into day
Honoring first sacred souls, guiding, delighting,
    intrinsically loving always

Palaces, concerts, playing, serenading
    greater I've ever known we simply give
Finding Elysian Fields, enlivening, endearing
    precious time we graciously live

Evolving, endlessly open, traveling, giving
    all others, sharing Gift of Life so true
Many long years, dreaming, wondering when,
    where, waiting patiently for you

(Written 1993)

WHEN SOME PEOPLE, I had been a consultant to, were very concerned with finding their mate, I would ask them to create an additional message related to their future soul mate to focus on, and repeat during the relaxation exercise. Maybe, because I still had to finish my manuscript, my mind hadn't been totally focused on finding my own love—soul mate.

Even much later, closer to the time of finishing my manuscript, I had a friend, who wanted to sell her house and live on the coast again. I asked her to pray, and to do her part to focus on "My house is now sold, and I am now always safe living on the coast again." I focused so intensely for her that it happened to me!

In February 1998, Tom and I were moving more of his things out of storage. We brought his valuable books that his grandfather and mother had written, and discovered a joyful surprise. His copy of *Judith of France*[54] had 4 *fleur-delis* on the cover of the book—like the gold pin that my great-grandmother had left to me! The copy I had borrowed from the library when I first met Tom didn't have this on the cover.

One morning in March, as I was waking up, I realized that I may not have worked enough with Tom on his letting go of the fear, pain, guilt and punishment from his past marriage, work and creativity.

Many of you may have had a lot of pain in your marriage and divorce. Even though you loved that person, that pain may also have been carried over into your work and creativity, sometimes one of the problems itself. You may have lost your balance between personal relationships, creativity and work creating another trap. You may have associated that you lost your relationship because of your creativity and work thereby creating fear and guilt.

Tom repeated the lines. "I am always safe letting go all fear, pain, guilt and punishment with myself, my past marriage, divorce, creativity and work when healthy for me." Then I asked him to repeat the statement, "I am always safe receiving and giving grace/compassion, love and peace to myself, her name, to marriage, divorce, creativity and work."

When he repeated the line, he began, "I am always safe receiving and giving *guilt*."—I stopped him and pointed out a problem—what had been hidden in his mind may have prevented greater closeness with me, and periodic blockage in his creativity and work. The fear was that when I am creative and work well, I may lose her. Also, important is to focus on "I'm always safe balancing my time each day, when healthy for me."

This may have been a problem for many of you when you separated, divorced or walked away from a relationship and went on to love again. You may have carried pain from your past experiences into your new relationships, many times blocking the very closeness and completeness, a true sense of belonging that you wanted. You may have feared getting very close to someone new because of your past inability to solve problems, and be close to someone you loved deeply.

The question many face is—*Am I able to solve problems in the present and not lose?*

On Friday, Tom and I left on our first adventure back to Santa Monica. Tom grew up there from the time he was 9 years old until he was 14, when he left for boarding school. I had lived in Santa Monica for approximately 10 years. Our first stop was at the house where Tom had lived when he was married and had his four children.

As we stood there, entering a time warp—I was feeling some of the pain of Tom's past experiences there. As we were walking around, we found our love filling our past memories, and soothing the loss we both had experienced, simultaneously loving being in present time. Now he is receiving added healing by pouring love into his past of mixed feelings as he is doing for me. While overlapping the past with our love in the present, we know we never have to lose love again. Now we can accept and give love more completely. This is possible because of the previous work we have already done through the letting go of fear, pain, guilt and punishment from our pasts creating more space and filling that space with love.

Then we drove to one of the medical treatment centers where I used to do consulting. As we walked around the area, my mind flooded with many memories of the years I had consulted in the different rooms for people and their families.

Next, we drove to where I used to live when I was married. I felt so happy to have Tom's love for me pouring through my own spaces of the past. We are both so happy to be together at last.

Let There Be

Let there be
While there's time to be free
To enjoy discovering mysteries
To see, hear and care
Touching moments we share
Joys balancing inner harmonies
Despair of wistful sufferings
Despair of hearts breaking, open
Openings uniting soul mates' searching journeys

Letting go
Giving space, let life flow
To fulfill unfolding destinies
Seeds of joy and pain
Growing seasons, cleansing rain
Peace, whispering sounds of being
Release of our suffering
Reveal the whys unknowing
Revealing, releasing becauses' hidden meanings

Love calls us free
Look within ourselves to see
To rejoice accepting memories
Gifts of calm and stormy nights
Learning to bend like the light
Tears—joys reflecting souls' discoveries
Flying with laughter
Joy flying again
Feeling Life lustrous higher than the Pleiades

Born to be
You and I were born to be

To unveil unspoken melodies
Time to give and receive
Reaching to you, you and I may be
Free, our love transcending galaxies
Grace is our giving
Grace is receiving,
Receiving, giving, floating fervent white lilies

(Written 1977)

We drove down to the 3rd Street Mall to have dinner at a Thai Restaurant where my daughter and I had dinner the previous summer in August to celebrate her birthday. This was right after I had first met Tom—completing a full circle of love.

That evening we drove to see my daughter performing in a play called "Hammergirl."[55] The play was magical! The beautiful musical telling a Norse myth seemed to reflect my own life of carrying a treasure (theirs a chest of jewels they were trying to exchange for peace to avert a war of revenge, and mine, this healing method to exchange for human lives to heal and give up revenge). The princess who had killed the Queen of the Trolls reminded me of people I consulted with—those in prison, and those I intervened for to keep them from going to prison. Although they had not killed anyone, they had harmed themselves and others. In consulting with people going to court, I gave (a form of exchange to the courts) a healing method for their lives to stop their personal war. A poignant line in the play—"You may have lost in the past. You don't have to go on losing."

The next morning we went out to breakfast with my daughter and her friend. This was another of those fun simple coincidences, as the day before I had pointed out to Tom that this would be a good place to eat breakfast with them. When they picked us up, I had forgotten the name of the restaurant, so they didn't know what restaurant I was referring to. They drove us to a place for breakfast and after parking, I looked up, and we were going to the same restaurant we had walked by the night before! We had a warm joyful time together sharing our lives together with our love story.

Then they drove us to what used to be Tom's grandparents' house. Tom had lived there from the time he was 9 until he was 14 with his mother, grandparents, older brother and sisters. This was also where his mother, a graduate of Radcliff, wrote all her books. Tom's grandfather, T.N. Carver had also authored many books. In one of his books, *Recollections of an Unplanned Life*,[56] he shares his delightful adventures of being a farm boy in Iowa. In 1882, he began his studies at Iowa Wesleyan University in Mt. Pleasant, Iowa, where he met Flora, his future wife. She went on to graduate, while he had to go back to work to help his family. Later he was sent to California to farm property his father had bought. He married Flora, and went back to finish college at the new University of Southern California, then in the countryside outside of Los Angeles. He went on to become Professor of Political Economy Emeritus at Harvard. He was a professor there from 1900 to 1930. Another interesting coincidence and connection is that Dr. David Baron who has served as a consultant for me all these years was born in Mt. Pleasant, Iowa.

My daughter and her friend left us to go on with the rest of their day's adventures. We had some time before lunch, so Tom took me to the place where his mother last lived before she passed away. We stood in the gardens and felt her spirit circling around us wafting in the winds through the trees, the sun sparkling my awareness. Then suddenly I saw on the side of the steps entering the front porch were tiles with a pattern of *four fleur-de-lis*, like the tiny gold lily pin my great-grandmother had left me—another circle complete.

We left to go to Venice to meet my writer friend, for lunch. I wanted Tom to meet him to include and share with Tom all aspects of my life that had led me to him. As I mentioned before, my friend had given me some suggestions for my manuscript around Thanksgiving in 1996. After carefully reviewing it several times, he had suggested that I reorganize the material from the simple to complex. He advised adding a chapter explaining double binds further, my discoveries, and new contributions to solving the problems. Then he gave me a chapter title, First Light," that came to his mind as he read my manuscript.

Then Tom and I went to the Santa Monica Library and found more of his mother's books—*The Secret of the Old House*[57] and *The Secret of the Closed Gate*.[58] These were somewhat biographical of Tom, his brother and two sisters when they were children and lived in the house in Virginia. In the library, I showed Tom the bookshelves where in 1995, while searching for R.D. Laing's and Gregory Bateson's books (checked out), I was spiritually led to *Synchronicity*[59] by F. David Peat which also eventually led me to Tom. I had read most of Dr. Peat's books to teach myself some of the language of physics. We also got books by R.D. Laing, F. David Peat, Ph.D. and John Briggs, Ph.D. Professor Briggs is the one who got me in contact with Dr. Peat in 1995.

We got on the freeway to drive back, and it was too crowded so we exited and rested. Then we began driving toward the ocean and realized we were close to where Tom's sister and brother-in-law live. Tom said let's call them. He called from our car, and his sister said to come right over for dinner. We had a wonderful time together. One of their sons was there, and their dog "Baudy" a Briard (French Sheepdog), who I met for the first time. Tom's sister told me Baudy is named after Baudoin Bras-de-Fer the knight that rescued Judith in the book *Judith of France*,[60] the book that led me to Tom—back full circle again. Tom said he had not known that Baudy was named after Baudoin Bras-de-Fer.

The following weekend on March 21, Tom had a chance to read more of some of David Peat's books.

When I awakened early on Monday morning, March 23, I had that electric feeling when a spiritual synchronistic experience is about to happen. The message came to me that it was time to call David Peat in London to make contact again because he may be going away. I didn't have his new London number. Luckily, earlier that month, I had chanced across the misfiled number of Dr. John Briggs, Ph.D. Two years before, he had assisted me to reach David Peat, communicating only by our message machines. This time John answered the phone himself. I told him that after his message reached me two years ago, I had contacted Dr. Peat, and that he had reviewed my manuscript. I explained that I was close to sending my revised manuscript to an agent, and needed to reach Dr. Peat again.

Three weeks later, I called Dr. Peat, and it was true! He said that in a couple of weeks, he and his family were moving to live in another country. He gave me his address, and agreed to read my revised manuscript and additional material.

From March through May, the days had continued with snow and cold, and I wondered when Spring would finally find us. We had set the date of May 24, to reaffirm our wedding vows with family and friends, at Willow Lake where we first met. With our families and friends all invited, we extended a pleading invitation for Spring to please join with us. We had had snow again just the week before, and the day before was gray, cold and overcast. When we woke up the next morning the skies opened to a beautiful crystal clear warm sunny morning, which stayed with us through our whole day of celebration until we left the party. Then the clouds moved back in again.

In the dancing sunlight of Spring, showering diamond sparkles on the alder, willow, oak and pine trees, we walked along the path of bright yellow daffodils, that family members and friends had planted in the years past, to stand on the place where we first met. Hillsides were filled with beautiful new bouquets, gentle breezes swaying softly all the Spring colors of wild flowers blooming.

Now we were surrounded by our families and friends to share with us as our brother performed the ceremony. There was a Maypole with long flowing colored ribbons, and we all danced together reminding me again of one of my favorite poems by e.e. cummings "when faces called flowers float out of the ground."

*when more than was lost has been found, has been
found all the mountains are dancing together*

Fours years after I moved to this beautiful area, the property was sold. Tom and I were able to stay a few more months, which coincided with the due date of this manuscript. We are very fortunate to have finished the editing of both books while living near where we first met. Then with very short notice, we were again spiritually led to another equally beautiful place to live in the mountains. There I completed my manuscript on a new, more visual, and fun method for beginners to learn to read music more easily. Tom and I are happily living, loving, working, writing, editing and teaching piano.

Twinkling Memories

Radiant year, graceful love seeds sown
Flowering from rags to riches we've grown
Rapturous memories of joy and care
Creating dazzling castles in mid-air
Squirrels and butterflies fluttering through our trees
Deer prancing, wild flowers frolicking windily free
This, the year you choose to be free
Your mind now clear—what is to be
Caressing truth, billowing breezes have blown
Trusting safety, you've found your true home
Softly in safety deeper truth truly known
Joyfully accepting wherever we've flown
Today, sunlight honoring, celebrating your birth
Timing your journey, meeting heaven on earth

Wafting illusions crown clear Summer air
Divining, declaring we've come through despair
Hearing the universe's cries of fear and pain
Swiftly we write sharing our messages of gain
Lucky we are, born clearly to see
Giving the gift to set all hearts free
Loving is a constant continuing continuum
Floating, expanding wave towards millennium
Winding crystal years 'round each others' hearts
Tenderly touching, sharing, we never will part
Released from flowering seeds we have grown
Cherishing this year we've divinely flown
Memories are twinkles of stars from afar
Gazing each evening, remembering who we are

(Written 1992)

The next chapter is a brief background of information on some barriers and solutions that may aid in feeling safe, comfortable with healthy comfort, and inner-healing.

[54] Leighton, Margaret, *Judith of France*, (Boston, Houghton Mifflin Company, The Riverside Press, 1948).

[55] Legawiec, Stephen, Playwright, Director, Co-founder of Gilgamesh Theatre.

[56] Carver, Thomas Nixon, Ph.D., LL.D., Litt.D., *Recollections of an Unplanned Life*, (Los Angeles, Ward Ritchie Press, 1949).

[57] Leighton, Margaret, *Secret of the Old House*, (Philadelphia, John C. Winston Co., 1941).

[58] Leighton, Margaret, *Secret of the Closed Gate*, 1944, (Philadelphia, The John Winston Company, 1944).

[59] Peat, F. David, Ph.D., *Synchronicity*, (New York, Bantam Books, 1987).

[60] Leighton, Margaret, *Judith of France*, (Boston, Houghton Mifflin Company, The Riverside Press, 1948).

16. PATHS TO CHANGE

* Do you think you and others deserve to enjoy your lives?
* Do you know all your time is valuable?
* Do you feel safe, or have you been just gutsing your way through life?
* Do you balance your time each day with healthy nutrition, exercise, rest, relationships, work and play? Do you enjoy all of these?
* Do you know, and feel that you and others are worthwhile and valuable 'just because!'?
* Do you have compassion for yourself and others?
* Do you safely and easily express yourself in some healthy form to let go of discomfort from the past, present or fear of the future?
* Have you been stuck in expressing your fear and pain, or are you able to let go of them, and go on to other wise, pleasant choices for your life?
* What are the thoughts and feelings that can aid you to do what you want that is wise and healthy?
* Do you enjoy loving and being loved—or would you like to?

DO YOUR ANSWERS TO the above questions show that you have been hurting yourself and maybe others? This book gives you a method that you can use to safely increase your knowledge, create new ideas, new perspectives, and change your behavior.

Inability to answer or resolve the above universal questions has blocked many from feeling and being safe with themselves and others—free from unnecessary excessive anxiety and stress. This explains why minor to major abuses and violence have been rampant in our world. In Chapter 17: Path of Discovery, I present a preventive and healing method with simple techniques using a new healthy perspective in logic. This addresses some of *the causes behind self-destructive behavior*, which may aid in *solving those problems*. Although people's logic is not always perfect, through this method we deal with the logic of paradox so everyone may benefit.

Since so many people have healed under many different circumstances and combinations of experiences related to prayer, diet, exercise, medical interventions, medical drugs, etc., it is important to have an openness to new possibilities, and be willing to experiment when wise and healthy for you. New information which may contribute to you feeling some safety to do this is a key issue.

Having the safety to know, create and make wise, healthy choices (including taking wise risks) may lead to the thrill of adventure. This includes your health, having enjoyable relationships, a job, creative fun, humor, etc. All these may affect your peace of mind and health.

When memorizing and applying the messages of this method presented in Chapter 17: Path of Discovery I, you may more easily release yourself from mental/emotional traps, and change barriers into open doors. With the messages of this method, you may now change your thoughts to reasons why and how you can transform your present and new relationships so you may have kind, caring people in your life:

Physicist, David Peat wrote about making changes:

> . . . It is equally possible to remain at the same job, in the same house, and with the same friends, and to exist in such a way that through a tiny shift in our way of encountering the world, everything appears fresh, new, and exciting . . .
>
> . . . When we respond to people in open, creative, and understanding ways, their attitudes toward us change, and the potential is present for something within them to change and open up, in turn.[61]

Some of you may think that you have to *want* to change before you are able. In the beginning, some people can't want to change, because they are lost in their confusion, overwhelming fear, pain, guilt or numbness, together with some hidden and known mental/ emotional traps that have kept them in confusion and darkness.

With this method using new perspectives in logic, you may more safely reach through (to yourself) with your new thought processes. Then you may more safely, clearly and easily see how to safely discover and release yourself from unnecessary traps, fear, pain, and guilt.

This book explains some simple reasons (which may seem surprising)—how you actually may benefit from the concepts of universal grace and compassion. These may aid you to resolve and release some double binds, and this actually may aid you in making more wise, healthy choices.

Why has it been that many of your choices turned out to be unwise and unhealthy, even when you may have known better? What blocked you? How can you choose to make and continue with many more wise, healthy enjoyable choices?

Barriers to Release:

There is a complex maze of interwoven problems (stressors) in language, thought, feeling, and behavior called "double binds," (mental/emotional traps). They are influenced by faulty logic, yet you can release yourself from them. Wise and healthy logic has its competitors—inner and outside interference and stress. Sometimes you may not have used your logic to make wise and healthy choices, you may have been blocked altogether, or deceived for a number of reasons, and this too, may have affected your health.

Although **double binds** are a problem for the **general population**, they were first described in 1956, by Gregory

Bateson, anthropologist, and colleagues, through double bind communication in schizophrenics.[62] Later, further complexities, and some novel techniques were described by Paul Watzlawick, Ph.D., psychotherapist, former clinical professor in the Department of Psychiatry at Stanford University, (since 1960, Senior Research Fellow at the Mental Research Institute, Palo Alto),[63, 64, 65, 66, 67] and Psychiatrist R.D.Laing.[68, 69]

Psychiatrist David Spiegel, M.D.,[70] also at Stanford Medical School, has described them in people having multiple personality disorders. More recently, Mony Elkaim, M.D.,[71] a neuropsychiatrist and psychotherapist, has discussed them in couples and family therapy. Kathleen Hall Jamieson,[72] Dean of the Annenberg School for Communication, University of Pennsylvania, has described double binds related to women's issues, including political viewpoints.

Gregory Batson, anthropologist and colleagues, R. D. Laing, M.D., Psychiatrist, and Paul Watzlawick, Ph.D., have written extensively on the double bind. Many barriers and double binds are discussed in *A Path to Light*.

Can you quickly release yourself from the fear, pain, guilt, or numbness in painful memories and present situations?

There is an additional problem, because sometimes when parents are inexperienced, they need to make so many choices for their children. Many children and young people grew up having little or no experience knowing and making wise, healthy choices (saying no to what is unhealthy, or saying no to too many healthy choices.) They also may not have understood that sometimes there can be short-term pain (discomfort) in saying no, or walking away from greater long-term pain. Additionally, sometimes the examples of choices made by their parents or guardians were unwise and unhealthy.

There have been other problems, even for some people growing up in relatively happy families. Sometimes they may not have had the experience of dealing with difficult people or situations. Later, they may have not clearly seen and listened clearly when choosing a partner (in life, marriage, work). Naively, they might have thought other people would be like their parents, relatives, siblings, or friends. Many people who grew up in unhappy families didn't learn to solve problems harmoniously to enjoy living, creating, playing, and working with others.

From confused thinking, people created universal problems called double binds. Just how thinking is done can be a solution,—or can be a problem, and affects creativity and knowledge. Early civilizations in attempting to prevent harm and pain to be safe, out of ignorance sometimes created reasons and stories that communicated painful mental/emotional traps. These are further discussed in my book, *A Path to Light*, Chapter 11: The Collective Subconscious.

Other Possible Factors In Healing

Another problem is the somewhat random fluctuation of nerve-signal transmissions in the biology of the nerves and synapses in the brain, which is just one aspect that contributes to variations of interpretations in thought processes. Also, the lack of precision in biological and psychological functions is another factor. In addition, because of stress, information may not have been accurately perceived or remembered, as well as all the details of the moments of a painful event, which may have resulted in misinterpretation.

All these factors, together with the various defense mechanisms, including "fight-or-flight," and some interwoven problems in language itself, created confusion (confused logic), and conflicts (mental/emotional traps). Add all these together with the problem that there are certain differences between the right and left hemispheres of the brain which process some information differently, and you may see and understand some of the complexities.

However, my method may give you some added simple tools to aid in more easily recognizing and solving these problems.

Effects In and On Memory

In 1991, it appeared that my method might also benefit Viet Nam veterans suffering from Post Traumatic Stress Disorder (PTSD). It was suggested to me that I contact Dr. Solomon at the Veteran's Administration (VA) Medical Center nearby, who then sent me many research papers. (I had already been using the method with cancer patients to quickly and more easily let go of unnecessary fear, pain, and guilt from *their* past painful and/or traumatic memories.) Months later in 1992, when some research funds were becoming available. I presented an abstract and description of the healing method I had designed to Dr. George Solomon, M.D., psychiatrist, then at VA Medical Center, in San Fernando Valley, Ca. and Professor of Psychiatry at the University of California at Los Angeles (UCLA). This convinced him to be a consultant on my proposed research grant.

An expert in the field of post-traumatic stress disorder with Viet-Nam veterans, Dr. Solomon mentioned that many of them seem to have been trapped in their pain for approximately 30 years. I then shared that I had been trapped for close to 35 years, and had found a way out. He immediately went to his file drawers, and began giving me many more research papers to assist me in my grant application. One that was of particular interest to me was an editorial related to PTSD titled "Conditioned Fear and Psychological Trauma." Through this paper, I was first introduced to the work of Joseph LeDoux, Ph.D., professor at the Center for Neural Science at New York University.

Dr. LeDoux concluded that, once formed, the subcortical traces of the conditioned fear response are indelible, and that *"emotional memory may be forever."* The editors concluded that PTSD may represent an unhappy human confirmation of this proposition.[73, 74]

In a recent telephone conversation with Dr. LeDoux in 1999, and again in 2001, he said he still thinks this may be true, but with new hope, and referred to his 1996 book, *The Emotional Brain.*[75]

> As things now stand, the amygdala has a greater influence on the cortex than the cortex has on the amygdala, allowing emotional arousal to dominate and control thinking . . . Telling yourself that you should not be anxious or depressed does not help much . . .
>
> Yet, there is another possibility. The increased connectivity between the amygdala and cortex involves fibers going from the cortex to the amygdala as well as from the amygdala to the cortex. If these nerve pathways strike a balance, it is possible that the struggle between thought and emotion may ultimately be resolved not by the dominance of emotional centers by cortical cognitions, but by a more harmonious integration of reason and passion. With increased connectivity between the cortex and amygdala, *cognition and emotion* (italics mine) might begin to work together rather than separately.

However, to deal with this cognition/emotion connectivity problem, the method I created initially *does* use aspects of cognition to dominate emotions in order to apply a pattern of a new healthy perspective in logical reasoning to the troubled mind. This may lead to a release from conflicting information and associations, along with the *multiple* double binds that up to then had been misleading some of your emotions causing further traps. While at first your painful emotions may still be out of control, this method gives you the tools to apply a new healthy perspective in logical reasoning by means of a new specific language patterning technique (later described in Chapter 17).

Some Solutions

This new perspective in logic and patterning addressing *multiple double binds*, may allow you to choose and accept more accurate information, and allow for the surfacing of new *different and sometimes formerly repressed constructive* thoughts and emotions.

By a guided repetitive pattern of specific thoughts and phrases with differing lag times, which address resolving, and/ or releasing conflicts, you may use a pattern of wise and healthy reasoning that may assist you to quickly gain control over particular thoughts and emotions. This may allow your harmonious emotions to surface. Literally and metaphorically, you may just stop beating yourself up, or banging your head against a wall (you may stop hurting yourself and others). Soon, with focused repetition, the healthy reasoning and harmonious emotions may become joined.

The result is that with increasing knowledge and understanding, along with the added thoughts and feelings of *safety* and *value* (self-worth), you may successfully accept new wise thoughts with decreasing resistance and lag-times. Through conscious repetition, new messages may become more second nature. The new needed connection patterns are gently exercised (as if by a nurturing parent), and you may develop new healthy response patterns. Through this method, you then may achieve a *cooperation* between cognition and emotions (cortex/amygdala) which may lead you to a more harmonious integration of reason and passion—more feeling, yet with a more healthy balance.

Because We Have The Gift of Life

Healing is here, when safely we see
Accepting the value of Life, we are free
Remembering times when we're spoken to
Remembering times when we we're led through
Now letting go fear and pain from our mind
Now changing thoughts to be sublime
Safe not hurting myself or others
Now so easy, we're sisters and brothers

Always safe letting fear and pain go
Now so easy, letting life flow
We're always safe receiving and giving
Now being wise, blissfully living
Receiving, giving Grace, Love and Peace
Now so easy we're healed and free
Come join this healing journey with me
We have the Gift of Life you see

One we are in Grace Love and Peace
Remembering flowers, their grace with ease
Millions and millions seemingly look alike
Standing there only, receiving, giving light
Their value and beauty, because they breathe
A new Loving Kindness for you and me
A new Life born, another traveling on
Our Lives continually, continue beyond

Only in Grace there is Love and Peace
Always safety, being you and me
Understanding, Forgiving, Universal Love
Eternal gifts, cascading from above
Knowing, living truth safely, we see
Grace is good will for you and me
Softly Grace on earth has come to be
Come join this healing journey with me

Next is the path of discovery I traveled to release myself and gain a high degree of inner peace and healing.

[61] Peat, F. David, Physicist, *The Blackwinged Night*, (Cambridge, MA, Perseus Publishing, 1000), p. 14.

[62] Bateson, Gregory, and Jackson, Don D., "Some Varieties of Pathogenic Organization." In David McK, Rioch, ed., *Disorders of Communication*, Volume 42, Research Publications. Association for Research in Nervous and Mental Disease, 1964, pp. 270-83.

[63] Watzlawick, Paul, PhD; Bavelas, Janet, Ph.D.; Jackson, Don, M.D.; *Pragmatics of Human Communication*, (New York, W.W. Norton & Company, Inc., 1967).

[64] Watzlawick, Paul, PhD, *How Real is Real?*, (New York, Random House, Inc., 1976).

[65] Watzlawick, Paul, PhD, *The Language of Change*, (New York, W.W. Norton & Company, Inc., 1978).

[66] Watzlawick, Paul, PhD, *The Situation is Hopeless, But Not Serious: The Pursuit of Unhappiness*, (New York, W.W. Norton & Company, Inc., 1983).

[67] Watzlawick, Paul, PhD, *Ultra-Solutions: How to Fail Most Successfully*, (New York, W.W. Norton, & Co., Inc.,1988).

[68] Laing, R.D., MD, *The Politics of the Family*, (New York, Pantheon Books, Random House, Inc., 1969).

[69] Laing, R.D., MD, *Knots*, (New York, Pantheon Books, A Division of Random House, 1970).

[70] Spiegel, David, MD, *Treatment of Multiple Personality Disorder*, Ch 3, "Dissociation, Double Binds, and Posttraumatic Stress in Multiple Personality Disorder," (Washington D.C., American Psychiatric Press, 1986), pp. 63-77.

[71] Elkaim, Mony, MD, *If You Love Me, Don't Love Me*, (New Jersey, Jason Aronson, Inc., 1990).

[72] Jamieson, Kathleen Hall, *Beyond the Double Bind*, (New York, Oxford University Press, 1995).

[73] LeDoux JE, "Information flow from sensation to emotion: Plasticity in the neural computation of stimulus value. In Gabriel M. Moore J (eds), *Learning Computational Neuroscience: Foundations of Adaptive Networks*. Cambridge, MA: MIT press, 1990, pp. 3-51.

[74] Shalev, Arieh; Rogel-Fuchs, Yael; Pitman, Roger; "Conditioned Fear and Psychological Trauma," *Society of Biological Psychiatry*, 1992; 31:863-865.

[75] LeDoux, Joseph, *The Emotional Brain*, (New York, Simon & Schuster, 1996), p. 303.

17. PATH OF DISCOVERY

Following is a list describing my path to healing:

1. First Light—Revealing answers
2. The Paradox of Safety. What is Safety?
3. Be Safe to be Wise
4. Think, Feel and Be Valuable.
5. Evidence For Your Worthiness
6. Untangle Contradictions With Grace/ Compassion vs. Punishment
7. Stop Hurting Yourself And Others
8. Being Safe
9. Let Go Of Fear, Pain, Guilt, or Numbness
10. Think and Feel Safe With Grace And Compassion

1. FIRST LIGHT—REVEALING ANSWERS

ONE EVENING, AS I sat alone in my living room, I reviewed my personal history. I remembered my spiritual experience of being led to study with a master concert pianist when I was 37 years old, even though I had only begun to play piano when I was 26. This was one of those wonderful experiences of receiving a blessing/opportunity, and I felt treated with dignity and respect. I compared this with the large number of painful, rejecting experiences I had up to that time.—And now I was facing Death.

Then I asked, "Why, after having been led all this way in a spiritual manner, now, just before my first audition with an orchestral conductor, would I lose my health, even my ability to play the piano, and maybe my life?" This question was the *first light beginning to shine on revealing answers.*

I became more aware that I had accepted the many distorted views I had been told about the way the world and people were and are.

When logic or reasoning has been based on invalid premises (untrue starting points) together with fear, pain, guilt, or numbness, it has been difficult (or seemed impossible) to make sense, and clear up confusion to let go of those feelings. This affects even *discovering, knowing and applying* wise healthy changes to get yourself to a personal goal. Many people, in different fields, have searched for reasons to bring safety, sense, order and harmony to ourselves and others. This method gives you a key as to how,—and some useful tools to apply.

For those of you who think you may not have a problem with safety, and may have been gutsing/charging through life with your fear and pain stored safely below the level of awareness, the following information on "safety" may apply.

Confused people had passed confusion on to me, just as it may have happened to you. This confusion had obstructed my discovery of how to let go of old fear, pain and guilt, and prevent more unnecessary pain. Knowing this along with the above example of receiving a blessing/opportunity gave me evidence that I too was valuable. Realizing this, I thought:

"Enough of this suffering! I don't deserve the suffering."
Then I made my few blessings and opportunities count more than my many painful experiences.

2. A PARADOX OF SAFETY

Many people learned to receive and give pain as a form of protection. I faced the reality that my being fearful and in pain had not always protected me from living in perpetual fear, pain, and guilt. I asked myself how could it hurt me to change and focus on the thought, *"I am always safe,"* even though I did not feel safe? Safety means to feel, to actually be protected from harm. Because I thought I was going to die, it seemed that no one could hurt me. I was finally able to stop worrying about being rejected. The small amount of pleasure and peace I had experienced in life came from what I thought of as a spiritual dimension with God, and some happy memories with my family, along with my recent underlying detachment from all people. I then felt a sort of (ultimate illusion) comfort, thinking about dying naturally in my sleep. I thought I had nothing to lose except fear, pain, and guilt. I felt an illusory sense of being safe. First came the thought, and then the feeling followed.

Another very important mental step I made was that since I had been safe when I listened and followed God and my inner constructive voice, I concluded that I am safe to live or to die. I thought death would be like sleep. I wouldn't remember leaving or where I had been. *In releasing my fear of death, it seems that death released me.* Feeling at peace about both life and death, together with focusing on the other aspects of this healing process resolved many of my conflicts and double binds. The high degree of inner peace (healthy comfort) that I was able to experience, I think allowed me to heal.

There is a *paradox* here. The safety and peace I felt as a result of my seeming detachment from life freed my mind to reflect on other issues of confusion and pain in my life. *Because I was free of fear, I was safe to ask questions, and then ideas came to me on how to solve these other issues.*

What is Safety?

You may not have a chronic disease, be facing death, or have issues of physical or sexual abuse. However, most of you may face fear/safety issues.

1. You may feel "unsafe" in a situation (or anticipated situation) when you have some expectations of painful happenings.

2. You may feel "safe" where the negatives were not reasonably expected, or you feel they are within what you could reasonably handle,—that is, not enough to matter.

3. You may have felt safe when you were not safe, or vice-versa.

As I succeeded with these issues in my own life, and later guided others by a more direct route, the pragmatic connection between somehow 'feeling safe' and dealing logically and effectively with these other problems became evident.

The 'feeling safe' mode
(How to achieve it is discussed later).

The following discussion takes into account some recent understanding about some of the many short steps and processing time-lags and overlaps involved in the sequences of thought-processes as consciousness and the brain absorb ideas. These processes and results are strongly affected by previously stored idea-patterns, and habits of emotional response. Learning certain new ideas and attitudes to replace established destructive ones is aided by suitably selected idea-patterns, repetitive phrase sequences, and language structure used in this method.

Judging a statement on whether you are safe or unsafe requires time for further assessment of the kinds and amounts of the perils—a delayed step before it can be negated. Therefore, in the later described guiding messages, the initial statement *"I am always safe . . ."* can stand briefly (without immediate rejection) during the short time while it and the next phrases are being absorbed. They are absorbed without being subjected to a quick logical rejection by the mind's *sometimes confused* logical censor, despite the mere known presence of some potential perils.

For example, the statement "I am always safe—"can be interpreted that in spite of dangers in the world around, I'm creating and attracting safety (from inner and outer sources). This is like focusing on: "My glass is half full," instead of " . . . half empty." As a result of having greater focused attention, necessary information comes to me on how to protect myself—because of this focus, I have greater awareness of when to take appropriate precautions, how to get what I want and need, and act accordingly. A simple example is when driving a car. Many times safe driving, and preventing an accident depend on a relaxed focused mind.

To enhance this logical acceptance of safety, . . . "when healthy for me" is added to any constructive message under focus. This reasonable added condition allows time for incorporating the whole complete statement, including some detail of what particular actions or regions of life the overall phrase is to apply. In this case related to safety—*to be safe is healthy, even when taking risks*. Sometimes you are safer taking a risk than staying where you are. I refer to this as outfoxing a paradox.

In honor of the healthy aspects of my defense mechanism, I worked in a creative way forming a partnership of healthy cooperation. Appealing to my mind's better nature, I gave examples of how we are safe, and the benefits of greater rational trust. I worked with my defense mechanism as countries sometimes do, cooperating for the overall benefit of spiritual peace, environmental responsibility and prosperity, rather than war. To modify years of a conditioned automatic rejecting response by my mind's defense mechanism. I compassionately and sometimes humorously showed it another way to live.

3. SAFE TO KNOW AND BE WISE

To resolve and untangle the tangle of another interwoven conflict associated with our self-worth and knowledge, I focus on the message . . .

"I am always safe living and being wise."

and . . .

"I am always safe learning and knowing what I need to know, when healthy for me."

These work together with the other messages of the healing method giving you a positive connection bridging between your healthy self-worth and the ideas *of being safe to live, learn, know and be wise.* (Wisdom also includes learning and knowing when and how you may safely express what you know.) Also an aid in solving the trap is to focus on and accept, *"I am Always safe, valuable, and cared for because I have the gift of life," (even when I don't know it all.)* Your evidences for this are that you are *here*, and you *have received* some *opportunities and blessings.*

These are messages that may replace the opposite messages in yourself, and may protect you from destructive messages and behavior. These may replace the contradictory messages and partial truths associated with danger and ignorance: that life is dangerous, and it is wrong to know too much. You can be safe even though there are dangers—you are safe to discover and know what you need to know.

This is important in letting go of fear, pain, guilt, and punishment, and to also let go of destructive messages associated *with living and learning—(TO KNOW).* You may have learned the following, which created painful conflicting mental and emotional traps:

1.   Life is dangerous, and it is wrong to know too much.
2.   In order to be valuable, you must always be right.

Examples of this are from a woman who told me:

> I don't feel 100% valuable because I should have known better than to get myself into a 'mess.' I have

been given a lot, and I should have the advantage to be able to succeed in most things. I was brought up that as a woman, I can't be too independent, or show I know very much. I also don't feel valuable because I did not do a really good job, a perfect job—and also because I wasn't always perfect.

Then I asked her what she thought or felt she needed to have or be, in order to be valuable. She said,

I need to be more present to others, not drifting off— I need to express my feelings, and let people know how I feel. I need to really get in touch with the real me inside and let that me show in the world.

Then I showed her a trap—how she thought the second list would somehow make her valuable. Next I showed her how she really is already 100% valuable because she exists, just like a newborn baby. Whether or not she is valuable, has nothing to do with her lists. She is 100% valuable just because she exists, *and may also feel* she should have known better . . . should have the advantages to succeed, didn't do a good job, and was not always perfect. She also is still 100% valuable, even when she isn't present, expressing feelings, and letting people know how she feels.

Through this transition of *knowing* you are valuable just because you exist, you may begin to *feel* more confident and valuable. The ability to enjoy yourself and others has nothing to do with actual value. What you do in life is how you are going take care of, and enjoy yourself and others—not prove your innate value. Yet when you think and feel valuable, you may go on to do what is valuable for yourself and others. She can also take care and enjoy herself and others by getting in touch with herself, expressing her feelings, being more present to others, and radiating in the world.

Some individuals have expressed that they haven't felt valuable when they expressed feelings of sadness, or any feeling other than happiness, (they felt wrong to feel sad, mad, etc). You may have found yourself in this mental/ emotional trap of low self-worth, and looked for any excuse to support how you were not valuable. This became a habit, and the game really was pain. You may have needed to continually look for reasons to play that game.

Through the self-worth work sheet, I showed her how she may lead herself out of the trap. She is 100% valuable, *and* she sometimes may or may not to do a good job, be perfect, express her feelings, get in touch with herself and radiate.

Not like a Robot!

Sometimes when appropriate, humor aids in changing a perspective. The following individual came to my public seminars:

He was a successful professional and bi-lingual. After I explained the method to everyone, he said he was concerned that he might become a robot if he used this method. I explained to him that he may already have been a kind of robot by obeying old commands which prevented him from being able to control his emotions through his own will. He laughed.

He said he didn't feel valuable because people criticized his ideas, and he felt he couldn't speak English very well. He also said he didn't want to feel valuable, because he didn't want God to think he was a snob.

I explained that he was valuable regardless of anyone's criticism. He was valuable whether or not anyone could see what he could see, or if they criticized what he did see. He actually spoke English better than he thought he did, and he is 100% valuable no matter how well he speaks. Even so, I pointed out to him that sometimes you may benefit when you can't explain yourself too clearly. Sometimes, in professional life, people can say too much too soon to the wrong person, and have their ideas taken and/or misinterpreted, and misrepresented.

I explained that to think and feel valuable are to *honor the life* you have been given as well as that of others. This frees your thoughts from the incessant preoccupation with weighing every thought, feeling, word, and action to determine your value. Instead, you can focus on creating, solving problems, working, and enjoying yourself and others. On the one hand he wanted people to value him, and on the other he thought he would be a snob if he valued himself. (See the trap!)

As to God's opinion of his value, I asked him to look at his pet. Do you value your pet as 7 or 10? Is there anything your pet must do to improve his value to you? He enthusiastically said no.

He went on to successfully use these ideas, and the other ideas of the healing method transforming his depression into happiness at will. His professional talks were well received, and he was going to begin traveling to speak in other places. Now he can enjoy himself and others.

4. THINK AND FEEL VALUABLE

The following explains a double bind problem that has prevented many from valuing themselves and others. Since it has been thought that it was wrong to know too much, it has been difficult to be right all the time in order to be valuable. Therefore it may have been difficult for you to feel valuable (have a healthy self-worth), or to know enough, gain, and/or understand enough accurate information to be valuable by that judgment scale. Right or wrong, knowing or not knowing have nothing to do with your innate value anyway.

Sometimes there can be an added problem in the interpretation of humility. Humility is honoring yourself, others, and life. Many of you may have felt guilty about learning and knowing, sometimes sabotaging yourselves. You may have noticed this problem in both followers and leaders.

You and all people are still valuable, although you may not have been treated as valuable by yourself and others, or you haven't treated others as valuable. We all have value just because we have the gift of life.

The following are examples of some of the misconceptions (confusing contradictions) of the truth that I had been taught from many different sources, and how I perceived, sorted out and untangled the contradictions involved.

I realized that sometimes God had led me, (because I listened and followed a thought, or feeling—a hint) and found myself in a special place, at a special moment in time, (a blessing-opportunity) even though I had made mistakes. For me, this was evidence that I (and all people) are valued and cared for just because we exist. I only had a few experiences of this up to that time. The main bulk of my experiences had been filled with pain and rejection.

From this evidence, I deduced that I wasn't being punished by God. I was being punished by myself and others. I realized that others, too, had been programmed like robots to receive and give pain to protect themselves. I made up my mind I was no longer going to let my value as a person be defined by them. In my mind, I began seeing, what seemed, my few experiences of blessings and opportunities as weighing more than the greater number of my painful experiences. I let my self-worth be defined by God, and my inner constructive voice. When I reflected on this I again experienced:

"I, you, and all people are always safe, valuable and cared for because we have the gift of life."

Some reasons as to *how I, you and all people are valuable* follow on pp. 210-211. You can focus on the evidence, and may convince yourself. Reflect on the above thought, and repeat this. Listen to what your thoughts say to you. Write down your insights. When you hear dissonance, (This is not the way I usually think, or arguments saying "Oh, no you're not. Who do you think you are?!"), educate yourself with evidence as to how you are valuable just because you have the gift of life. Pay attention to your experiences, reread the message, reflect on the evidence, value it—use it to defend yourself and others as though you are a defense lawyer,—that is—take nurturing care of yourself and others.

Many people have felt that, because they were sick, they must have done something bad, and were being punished. They made a condemning judgment against themselves that somehow they must be terrible people, and also felt guilty because they had an illness. They felt they were not valuable. There are many variables that contribute to a person being vulnerable to illness. In addition, some people feel they don't want to be a burden to others when they are sick. I reminded them that when they were children and sometimes ill, most of them were taken care of by their parents, and if they themselves had children, they probably took care of them when they were sick. No matter what, if you happen to have an illness, it is your turn to receive care. Ask yourself—"What are my problems, and how can I solve them? How can I take control of my life?" You may find it helpful to ask questions before falling asleep, and you may awaken with some wise solutions.

Multiple Personality Disorder (MPD)

In one of my public seminars in a psychiatric hospital, I gave an unusual demonstration of how accepting the concept of . . .

We are all safe, 100% valuable, and cared for because we have the gift of life"

. . . can be beneficial and healing with another problem.

In my seminars I ask people to fill in a self-worth work sheet and another questionnaire. After completing the forms, I

asked those who would like to participate to tell how valuable
they thought and felt on the scale of 1 to 10—(1 being low and
10 being high).

When they responded with any number less than 10, I
asked them to write down their reasons, and those who wanted
to share could do so. After hearing each person, I showed how
a mental/emotional trap may be in their thoughts and feelings,
and how they might free themselves.

Eventually, I came to one lady who said she felt like a 1,
and after talking with her, she then added Mary felt a 2, and
soon after our discussion she added that Jane felt a 4.

Suddenly I realized that she had a multiple personality
disorder (MPD). I showed her how to release the trap of low
self-worth to feel valuable by each of her personalities, and
how to be safe to not hurt herself or others. This might give her
a safer healthy control. She participated in the group relaxation
exercise. I had read that people with MPD have developed
one or more abusive personalities in order to gain control—to
try to feel safe, since their abusive model or models had had
control over them.

David Spiegel, M. D., psychiatrist, stated that in cases of
people with MPD . . .

> They maintain a sense of separateness by having
> secret personalities who are experienced as
> independent of parental control. Indeed, these
> patients often enhance their sense of control by
> identifying with the aggressor, the abusive parent.
> One or more of the dissociated personalities often
> inflicts physical harm in the same way that the
> parent did, conveying a false sense of mastery over
> the physical abuse.[76]

As we can see, although people with MPD have needed one
or more abusive identities for an illusion of safety, they were
not really safe at all. Solving and releasing some interwoven

mental traps, and feeling 100% valuable are some of the steps to have control to be safe without abuse. Later, other steps are discussed which include resolving other mental traps, and doing the repetitive work of accepting safety while letting go of fear and pain using particular messages woven with safety.

Schizophrenia

The following person had been diagnosed with paranoid schizophrenia.

Like many people, he also had a problem with not feeling valuable. He said that he didn't know that God would listen and help him. He thought God was too big and busy, and he was too small. I explained that if God didn't listen to him and others, God would be unemployed. He laughed. I explained how we are all valuable, and led him through the steps of the healing method. He said his goal is:

"I will (future tense) like to find some way to help and communicate with the people."

I explained about the use of verb tenses to aid in communicating more directly. I gave him some examples of how he could change the above statement to the present tense—"I am always safe finding ways to help and communicate with people when healthy for me," or "I am always safe helping and communicating with people when healthy for me." I also explained that he may think of other choices himself.

He also told me that he would get in trouble at work, and sometimes lose jobs because he would stop to talk with the good voices that he enjoys. I explained that he could carry a note pad in his shirt pocket. When the good voices begin to talk to him, he could jot down a few notes, and tell them he would meet with them after work to talk.

As to his yelling voices, I explained that he could give them grace, love and peace, to teach them another way. He would be replacing his former painful reactions with his constructive attention and love. He experimented with all of these ideas, as well as used my relaxation tape. He said that when we were doing the relaxation exercise together, as well as when he used my cassette tape, the bad voices didn't yell at him. In a few weeks, he found greater peace and joy.

5. EVIDENCE FOR YOUR WORTHINESS

Many of you may not have a disease, such as cancer, and instead may feel depressed or anxious. Ask yourself, "Was I 100% valuable even when I was ill? Are your loved ones valuable even when they are ill?" A wise answer is "yes." What is your answer? You may change it to a "yes."

Other evidences to support the conclusion that you and all people are valuable are to look to *nature—trees, flowers, animals, sky, stars,* etc. Our reaction is *"how wonderful, just because they exist."* What does the energy of new life into the world say to us? ***Our value based on "beingness" is shown when a baby is born.*** A baby can't do much, and yet we value and celebrate this new life. This, as well as other blessings and opportunities we are given, are evidences.

It is not only shown through the experience of new life—also even the *loss of someone you love may lead you to recognize and feel the value of life.* Therefore I concluded "We all are valuable because we have the gift of life."

You can also silently receive and give grace, love and peace to yourself and others which is a grand gift to receive and give to others.

Many people *learned* the need to receive and give pain (punish and reject), as a result of their own fear and need to protect themselves. Because of this need, I reflected upon the fact that people had searched for, and created reasons to make hurtful judgments in order to carry out rejection—created an illusory or real distance (form of safety). Those caught in this trap may have acted out a form of self-sabotage.

People had acted out this behavior rationalizing it with using trivial to serious reasons. I then focused on the message *"We are always safe, valuable and cared for because we have the gift of life."*

Some people have been afraid this was arrogance. This created a conflict. One way out of this conflict is to view that when you value yourself and others, this is honoring and having humility for the value of all life. You may have noticed that when you value a book or car, you take better care of it. When people think and feel valuable they go on, and have clearer thoughts and feelings to choose and do what is wise and healthy.

6. UNTANGLING CONTRADICTIONS WITH GRACE AND COMPASSION

As I was in concentrated thought, suddenly, I experienced two insights that changed my direction in thought. In making the following observation of the meanings of grace and compassion, I was able to make distinctions through looking at those meanings, applying a new perspective in logic, and made the necessary adjustments in my thinking to accept these concepts into my life—a process called learning (to come to know).

I thought about the concepts of *grace and compassion*. Grace is mercy, forgiveness, and unmerited love. *Compassion* is to have deep sympathy for the sufferings of another with an urge to help. I realized that I had learned a restrictive form of *"selective* grace and compassion." This meant I could only receive grace and compassion under certain circumstances.

Very rarely, had I been able to temporarily receive and give grace and compassion to myself. I found it easier to give grace and compassion to others, I understood they were unable to help themselves. Sometimes this happened even during extremely stressful circumstances, even when others knowingly or unknowingly were trying to harm me, and also to those people who had good intentions. I never wished anyone harm, and sometimes was just too preoccupied with my own pain. I had been so absorbed in and overwhelmed by my own fear and pain that I had been unable to solve the problem of how to have grace and compassion for myself all the time. I felt others deserved it. I was confused with punishment vs. grace for myself, and how to stop the pain from memories. Having selective grace for myself hadn't stopped the pain from memories, or from allowing myself to be hurt by others. At that time, I was not aware that included in grace for others is to accept it for myself. Another act of grace is *alleviating the pain of others* who have been hurting from seeing me hurt. That was an area of grace that I had missed.

> *By accepting universal grace and compassion for myself,*
> *I am also giving it to others.*

Using grace and compassion in a restricted way had created a separateness, a wall of distance within myself and between myself and others. My additional evidence for universal grace and compassion came when reflecting upon my few experiences of being led by God through my thoughts, and had received opportunities and blessings. I realized that since the spiritual dimension had led me, (and I listened and followed) to be in a place to receive and give, that this is further evidence that I (and all people) are valued and cared for just because we exist—grace in action. I only had a few examples at that time. I realized that God was not punishing me. I had only been allowing myself and others to punish me, as I didn't know at that time how to prevent it.

7. HOW TO STOP HURTING YOURSELF AND OTHERS

One evening, when I was so ill, just before falling asleep I asked God,

"What is missing from the thoughts of people who do not do what is best for themselves?"

In the middle of the night, I was awakened with a voice through my thoughts that said,

"It's very simple"—

"I am always safe NOT HURTING myself, you, or others with any fear, pain, guilt or punishment associated with myself, mother, father and _____ (others) when healthy for me."

Every night, I repeated this message at least 4 times before falling asleep, as well as some other messages of my healing method mentioned in Chapter 8.

A crucial piece of the puzzle had been revealed to me.

I then realized that many people, as well as myself, had learned to receive and give pain as a form of protection (to hurt oneself and others). *This is the opposite to "not hurting oneself or others."* Through using the above message, *now change is possible.*

Suddenly, I had an image of the menu on a computer that has a missing or hidden line. You usually can't notice it when it is not there, or you may have a blind spot because of negative programming. This explains one of the reasons why some haven't seen this missing or hidden thought, or ignored it. You may have been fitting into (cooperating with) an illusory form of self-protection (obeying a destructive 'self-protection' program). This explains why many may have continued hurtful behavior even after knowledge and/or punishment of such unnecessary and hurtful behavior.

*My mind was then open to receive
other positive messages.*

When you accept "safe not hurting myself or others when healthy for me" your thoughts may then accept and cooperate with other positive messages.

As a result of the past influences "to hurt oneself and others," the message . . .

"when healthy for me and/or us"

. . . may also have been missing from the minds of many people.

"When healthy for me and/or us," a related, conditional rider-phrase, is added to the end of most of the messages of this healing method. When you have made choices, you may have rarely stopped to think and ask yourself, *"Is this healthy for me and others?"* Thus, harmful behavior may have resulted. Adding "when healthy for us," aids you to remind yourself to think, feel and do what is healthy for you and others (which aids you in prevention—one of the effective goals of healing). The resultant choices are then appropriate in widely varying circumstances.

This conditional rider-phrase also acts as a qualifier which allows new healthy thoughts to be accepted and not be automatically rejected (censored by confused logic, as well as a logic that may not have seen the whole picture). Because of the problem of unresolved experiences of past fear and pain, the sometimes confused logical defense mechanisms may have kept you from either knowingly or unknowingly making wise healthy choices.

Freud called it . . .

. . . knowing and not-knowing, a state of rational apprehension that does not result in appropriate action.[77]

I Am Always Safe?

When the new message *"NOT HURTING MYSELF OR OTHERS WHEN HEALTHY FOR US."* is accepted, you may be alerted to make many more healthy choices. There is a *paradox* in that sometimes there may be *short-term fear and pain* in walking away from or letting go of *potential long-term fear and pain.* Many times people are just tolerating a painful situation, or are numbed to an extent by their fear and pain. Both may be temporarily trapped by real, imagined or inappropriate feelings of guilt. For some, having fear and pain created an illusion of safety, strange as this sounds. You may have learned that you are selfish when you take care of yourself. You may not have realized that when you take care of yourself, you can do more with and for others. Also, the thought of doing something different may have conjured up the fear that others may create more pain (life may be worse) rather than (life may be better). When you hurt yourself, then others are also hurt.

For those of you who may have difficulty focusing on this new thought for your own sake, you may be inspired to focus, for the sake of others, on the following thought:

> *"I am always safe not hurting myself (or others) for*
> *others sake when healthy for me."*

8. BEING SAFE—Along with "I am always safe not hurting myself or others when healthy for us," I focus on:

"I am, you and all people are always safe."

This is not a "Pollyanna" idea. Just because the above statement itself may temporarily seem untrue, does not mean it *is* untrue! Some people have said to me, "I may be safe and you may be safe. Don't tell me all people are safe." Even though you have experienced a lack of safety, dreaded some future experience, or real or imagined threats, you can change your point of view. You may create safety in what may seem or be a potentially unsafe situation, (protect yourself from unsafe situations) by having and acting on clearer perceptions. The following explains how.

Self-protection

For me, there is a form of self-protection in concentrating on the concept of *"We are always safe."* This awareness allows me to bring forth the safety in myself (how to protect myself), and attract safety from others and circumstances. I, other people, and circumstances seem to come and go to protect me *creating a safety field.* Also, when I let go of fear and pain from the past, I increase my safety because I don't distract or hurt myself with the pain of the past anymore. Instead, I create a safety field of good will thoughts, even when I may have some anxiety or fear about a present situation. With this view, even when others may have hidden or known harmful aspects, by having greater inner peace and awareness, I protect myself, thereby creating a safer situation. Other people have a choice, so either the situation transforms at the time, or I walk away respecting the other people's situation. I can say no to harmful behavior, and receive and give grace, love and peace in my thoughts and behavior. Other people may or may not transform at that time.

Safe Even With My Car

This doesn't mean that I drive late in the evening when I have another choice, and stop locking the doors in my car. Although in Los Angeles, I did have an experience of forgetting to lock the doors on my car. The next morning there was a note on my car from someone requesting to buy my car. Also, whenever my car has had a problem causing it to unexpectedly breakdown, it has always happened in front of a car repair place even though I drive hundred mile distances.

One person, from my seminars, reported to me that late one evening, he was walking down Western Avenue in Los Angeles, and a man jumped out of a car and came toward him with a gun to rob him. My client had learned my method, and said another car with young men saw him, stopped, jumped out of their car and scared off the potential robber. I don't know whether this will happen in all cases.

Many people have been so locked into fear and pain, they seemed to have lived only in the dimension of **"I am."** They may have only been concerned with their own fear and pain, and not very aware of others. Focusing on **"I am, you and all people are always safe,"** together with the other messages of this healing method may make it possible for you to safely move yourself into a dimension of greater awareness of yourself and others (yourself, a close personal relationship, and all people) with the universal concepts of grace and compassion.

Then focusing on the thought, "I am always safe not hurting myself, you, or others when healthy for me," as well as the previously mentioned thoughts may be some beginning steps for you to be able to make additional new wise healthy choices and changes. Each person in a relationship may benefit when focusing on these new thoughts, including "not hurting yourself or others." Then you and others may think of, and follow through with harmonious, healing interactions.

It may not be necessary for people to experience a painful accident, chronic illness, to be near dying, or desire to die in order to create the healthy changes I made. Also, it may not be necessary to leave those people you either care about, or have cared for, through separation or divorce in order to make healing, loving changes.

9. LETTING GO OF FEAR, PAIN, OR NUMBNESS

Because of focusing on, and *doing adequate repetitions* to integrate "I'm always safe not hurting myself or others when healthy for me," my mind was then ready to focus on and accept the following message:

"I am always safe LETTING GO OF FEAR, PAIN, GUILT, AND PUNISHMENT associated with myself, mother, father, (others), food, liquids, money, and receiving and giving love when healthy for me."

I no longer need the fear and pain from the past to protect myself. I protect myself with the information from my past, as well as through the concept of safety and grace, love, and peace. Also, I let go of fear and pain faster in present situations and fear of the future by changing my thoughts.

Why has there been a tendency to hold on to painful thoughts, feelings, and behavior? Perhaps, it may have originally served as a protective defense—a way of controlling against repeating the actions that had led to painful emotions and behavior from which you were trying to protect yourself. You might not have been aware of being trapped in fear, anger, sadness, etc. in attempting to avoid possible humiliation, rejection or physical harm.

You may even have distracted yourself with excessive activity, overworking, shopping, procrastination, or escaped into overeating, excessive drinking, etc. as an unhealthy form of self-nurturing. As a result you may have ignored fatigue and deprived yourself of affection.

Comfort and Immune System

There has been speculation that sometimes the expression of anger and grief may have a positive effect on the immune system. One research paper states, "the subjects who showed the greatest degree of immune changes were those who reported less depressed and anxious mood states, but more anger."—But it also goes on to state:

> However, the [qualified] endorsement of anger appeared to group leaders, in fact, to be an expression of *assertiveness* and *defiance*, rather than irritability or rage.[78]

In other words, the form of anger, which the patients expressed was *assertiveness* and *defiance* which (together with less depression and anxiety) somehow led to aiding their immune system.

It may be likely that the above mentioned assertiveness or defiance, although motivated by anger (or other mood states such as grief), may move you to constructive thoughts, feelings and/ or do wise healthy *actions* which may create greater feelings of *comfort*. It is this comfort that may be the "somehow" which has a healthy effect on the immune system. Doctors find comfort is a potent medicine.[79]

Also, there are other mood states, other than anger and grief, *such as discomfort, grace, compassion, love, etc.*, which may more comfortably move you to be assertive to find greater comfort as further described in this chapter.

In my case, continuous expression of my grief, or trying to conjure up anger had not been solutions.[80] I had done enough grieving. For me, many times sadness had been a habitual response to every situation that I did not expect or anticipate.

Justification For Letting Go

Also, I realized that we all can manage to find some sort of justification for grieving and being angry in every moment about the injustices that have been done to ourselves and others. At some point in time, letting go of pain from the past may be wise and healthy. Many physical wounds heal and we go on, forgetting the pain. Sometimes we do have a choice as to how long we want to grieve or feel any other emotion.

One person with a serious illness told me the following:

> "I'll admit to anger, a great deal of it, but it is not directed at a loved one, and unfortunately cannot be dissipated until I receive some vindication. That will probably never happen. Some of my friends have tried to change this attitude, but on learning why I have this feeling, they all agree with me."

When she told me that she was not interested in letting go of her anger because she wanted vindication, I explained to her that *one of her vindications is in letting go of her anger* so she can feel better. This makes practical sense, since, as she said vindication from the other person may never happen.

10. HOW TO THINK AND FEEL SAFE WITH GRACE AND COMPASSION

In 1979, I was told through my thoughts to silently focus on the following message whenever I was in the presence of anyone who is anxious or upset. Also, I was told to focus on this thought for people who are a long distance away. I included this in the method:

> *"I am always safe receiving and giving grace, compassion, love, and peace to myself, mother, father,*
> *_____(others), and all people."*

Silent Communication

Everyday, I focus on this "silent" gesture of good will, repeatedly in the presence of anyone, to anyone who may be at a distance, and to anyone who may be angry, sad, ill, discontented, or even happy. This is also important when remembering people who have passed away. You may still resolve your conflicts with them and gain peace.

There are times when people are not reachable through the audible voice. There has been so much attachment to pain through the voice. Sometimes, just focusing on the thought can be more effective in reaching others than through audible speech. Again, to make this easier, I remember that others' fear and pain may have been, or may be greater than my own.

In the beginning, you may not feel or be entirely sincere, because of some fear or pain, such as a lingering resentment toward one or more people who are or have been important in your life. For instance, often even well into one's adult years, there may be mixed-thoughts and feelings towards one's parents and others. Through repeating the above message by rote, you may integrate this concept into your thoughts, feelings and behavior. Then you may resolve your ambivalence, and release it. You still may not want to be with them depending on circumstances.

In essence, this message is a prayer for their healing.

Some people have been afraid that if they did send good will silently through their thoughts to those who have harmed them, that they, themselves, would soften, and contact whoever may have hurt them. Contact with others is not necessary to gain a release. If you know that they no longer want to hurt you, you may want to contact them. If they are still trying to harm you, you don't have to have contact with them, or you may think of new creative ways to relate to them. Again, it is not necessary in order to gain a release.

The positive benefit for you, in sending your silent thoughts of grace, compassion, love and peace to others, is that you don't have to block yourself from enjoying life. You can let go of unnecessary numbness, sadness, resentment, or anger, which may have colored the rest of your other experiences with yourself and others.

When you realize that other people also knowingly or unknowingly have experienced ignorance, fear and pain, then compassion may be easier for you to give to others.

Because receiving and giving grace and compassion made logical sense to me, I was sincere, in that it made intellectual sense, although at first, I wasn't able to feel the deeper implications of the process I was entering. My fear and pain were blocking my feelings of grace and compassion. By rote, I repeated the above messages in my relaxation exercise. Intermittently throughout the day and evening, I also focused on the messages.

Unexpectedly, 10 days later my fear and pain were gone. My intrusive repetitive thoughts and feelings of fear and pain from the past ended.

After two more additional weeks of repeating this method, unexpectedly, I was in remission. All my physical painful symptoms had disappeared. A later study on older adults in independent living facilities showed that only those subjects in the relaxation condition demonstrated (through blood tests) improvement in immune function.[81]

Frequent Questions

In my public seminars, one frequent question would be asked: What about in traffic, when someone cuts in front of me? Can I send grace and compassion with a snarl? I said think it from whatever mental/emotional space you are in at the present time. Then feel yourself float into a better disposition than when you first started with a snarl. When repeatedly using such an approach, you may be a healing gift for yourself and others.

What may have prevented you from experiencing the most natural and beautiful gift of life: that of enthusiastically caring for yourself and others? This is true aliveness—to really care deeply, without needing to hold back. However, past experiences of fear and pain may have produced powerful negative memories, which were often associated with people and activities that you would have otherwise enjoyed. Your discomfort may have led to emotional distance, frequently as a form of self-protection. Not only did you not enjoy your close relationships, you may have preferred people you didn't see often, or who were at a great physical distance. Were you avoiding close, intimate contact?

Some of you may have been afraid that grace and compassion may put you in the presence of others with whom you have felt or feel uncomfortable. This is not the case. You have a choice. It may not be necessary to be in that person's presence. Thoughts of grace and compassion may provide an aura of protection, with love and healing projected onto yourself and others. This also, provides a beautiful experience of thinking, and praying "silent thoughts," creating the space for the potential of healing for yourself and others.

There is another dimension to this—When you may be "at home" in this realm, you may be at home in the presence of all others, whether or not they share the same perception. Grace—sharing—You may reach out with thoughts and prayers of grace regardless. You may feel and be in grace even when others are not able.

Cooperation in grace and compassion may be needed to bring people together in a healthy way. There are people with varying degrees of destructive tendencies, who you have been meeting on your path anyway. Your *lack* of grace and compassion probably hasn't protected you.

All people deserve rehabilitation and healing.

This may be the essence of your own change, your own healing. When you realize that other people's ignorance, fear and pain may have been like yours, or greater than your own, then grace and compassion may be easier for you to give to others.

(It may also be beneficial that you even have grace and compassion for those with lesser ignorance, fear, and pain, etc. than your own!)

When I was ill, I would relax one area of my body at a time, repeating all the messages of this method at each place, while lying down. Also at the same time, with my imagination, I focused on feeling a pulse, and sending healing twinkle star cells to each part of my body even though I didn't have faith that this would work.

Also, I allow myself to think and feel protected by Grace, and continue to ask God for guidance.

You may experiment, see, and experience the results you get from silently receiving and giving grace, compassion, love, and peace. For further information read *A Path to Light: How to Not Not Make Healthy Choices.*

76 Spiegel, David, MD, *Treatment of Multiple Personality Disorder*, (Washington D.C., American Psychiatric Press, 1986), p. 73.
77 Gay, Peter, *Freud, A Life For Our Time*, (New York, W. W. Norton & Company, Inc., 1968), p. 427.
78 Fawzy, Fawzy I., MD, Kemeny, Margaret E., PhD., Fawzy, Nancy W., RN, MN, Elashoff, Robert, PhD, Morton, Donald, MD, Cousins, Norman, Fahey, John L., MD, "II. A Structured Psychiatric Intervention for Cancer Patients," *Arch General Psychiatry*, Vol. 4, August 1990, p. 734.

[79] Goleman, Daniel, "Doctors Find Comfort is a Potent Medicine," *Science*, November 26, 1991.

[80] Irwin, Michael, MD, "Depression May Reduce Activity of Natural Killer Cells," *Research Resources Reporter,* Volume XIII, no. II, November 1989.

[81] Kiecolt-Glaser, J., Glaser R., "Psychoneuroimmunology: Can Psychological Interventions modulate Immunity?" *Journal of Consulting and Clinical Psychology*, 1992, Vol 60, No 4, pp. 569-575.

Lost is a Place Too

Lost is a place too
Dawning insights, life renews
Knowing your way through
Life sparkles anew
Feel compassion, feel love
Feel grace from above
Now I am here with you
Lost in a Universe, we, too

Lost is a place too
Finding how is where you
Release your fear, letting go pain
Seeing inside, feeling the gain
Safely to love, peace softly falls
Miracles descending now to all
Receiving, giving, being with you
Lost together our souls renew

by Judy Leighton

APPENDIX

PREVENTION & HEALING KIT

THE PROBLEM SOLVER KIT gives you the tools, which includes an Emergency Work Sheet, Self-Worth Exercise, and a Self-evaluation Form.

These may aid you to more easily recognize, and release mental/emotional traps.

This method may aid you to feel and be safe with constructive changes in your thinking and behavior, through simple techniques. They allow you to accept the concept of safety to gain the knowledge and wisdom to resolve some multiple double binds, and reinterpret the past, present and future. This makes it possible to more easily let go of fear, pain or numbness, and make *lasting healthier wise choices*. With this safety you know that somehow you can handle whatever changes you make, and deal with whatever comes.

This method may also aid you to accept that you are valuable. This interrupts a double bind (interwoven with some others) that was based on a value system that viewed one as more or less valuable, or not at all, depending on many temporary fluctuating factors. These changes, in your thoughts and understanding about the past, further effect changes in your perceptions about the present, and the future. My website is www.apathtolight.com.

FOR PEOPLE WHO THINK THEY MAY BE IN A CRISIS OR EMERGENCY SITUATION.

(See next two pages)

EMERGENCY WORK SHEET

If problems with your food/appetite, you can think "I'm always safe drinking and eating slowly what is healthy for me." One client, after 3 days of not eating, chose to drink organic peppermint tea—then soon chose some favorite healthy comfort food.

You can focus on the following messages in your thoughts (4 times each) anytime—on waking, during the day, and before falling asleep. This frees you to experience greater comfort, healing and wellness.

The first two basic messages that may have been confused, hidden, or missing from many people are:

I am always safe *knowing and living truth*
when healthy for me.

I am always *safe not hurting myself, you,
or others* when healthy for me.

The second message may have been confused, hidden, or missing because many people's over-active defense mechanisms have been based on fear and pain—hurt oneself and others for protection. It is vital to focus on the above opposite message, which may aid you to gain safety, comfort and a healthy pace. You can now protect yourself within the concept of safety. When you may be uncomfortable with yourself, what people say, or do, or situations, you can now quickly focus on the messages listed below, allowing yourself to change your thoughts, feelings and behavior to comfort. You can relate to people and situations that can be resolved, and/or walk away with dignity and respect for all. Look for how everyone benefits.

In the beginning, you may or may not be sincere, or feel the meaning of the thoughts you are repeating. Sometimes your fear and pain may be in the way. You may benefit when you repeat the following thoughts by rote. (This method worked for me and others.)

MAIN MESSAGES

1. I am always *safe knowing and living truth* when healthy for me.
2. I am always *safe not hurting myself, you, or others* with any fear, pain, guilt and punishment with myself, mother, father, _____ (anyone else), and all people when healthy for me.
3. I am always *safe living and being wise* when healthy for me.
4. I am always *safe learning, knowing, and doing* _____ when healthy for me.
5. We are always *safe, valuable and cared* for because we have the gift of life.
6. I am always *safe letting go of fear, pain, guilt, anger, sadness, and punishment* with myself, with mother, father, _____ (anyone else), and all people when healthy for me.
7. I am always *safe receiving and giving grace, compassion, love and peace* to myself, mother, father, _____ (anyone else) and all people when healthy for me.
8. We (my family, friends, others, and I) are *always safe, protected, and healed* when healthy for us.

Message No. 1 and 2 alert you that you are beginning a process of a new thought and behavior pattern of safety.

Now you may cooperate, and let go of fear, pain or numbness when it is healthy for you. You can use your new awareness for greater access to your intuition, knowledge, as well as comfort to protect yourself. When you are relaxed, you have more access to all your senses, and greater clarity to be protective in a healthy manner.

ADDITIONAL KEY MESSAGES OF THIS METHOD

1. We are always safe letting go of fear, sadness, anger, worry, frustration, and loneliness when healthy for us.
2. We are always safe not blaming or judging ourselves, mother, father, _____ and all people when healthy for us.
3. We are always safe forgiving ourselves, mother, father _____, and all people when healthy for us.
4. We are always safe living and sharing together in mutual understanding, grace, compassion, forgiveness, trust, love, peace and joy when healthy for us.

The messages I integrated gave me self-control over my thoughts, feelings and actions that produced a high degree of healthy comfort and peace, which may have been a factor that allowed me to heal. Having the ability to control and comfort oneself to gain peace are very important ingredients to healing.

ADDITIONAL KEY MESSAGES FOR WEIGHT-LOSS,
LETTING GO SMOKING, DRUGS, AND ALCOHOL,
CANCER, AND ARTHRITIS

5. I am always *safe knowing, finding, and doing* the healthy treatments for me.
6. I am always *safe losing weight* when healthy for me.
7. I am always *safe weighing* _____ *lb.* when healthy for me.
8. I am always *safe eating and drinking slowly*, what is healthy for me.
9. I am always *safe exercising and walking* when healthy for me.
10. I am always *safe letting go of smoking* when healthy for me.
11. I am always *safe letting go of drugs and alcohol* when healthy for me.

12. I am always *safe sending healing twinkle star cells to my* _____, when healthy for me.
13. I am always *safe letting go of* the pain, stiffness, and swelling in my _____, when healthy for me. (this is what I added for myself re arthritis).
14. We are always *safe protected and healed* when healthy for us.

KEY MESSAGES FOR RELATIONSHIPS AND MONEY

For existing relationship:

We are always safe living and sharing together in mutual understanding, grace, compassion, trust, love, peace and joy when healthy for us.

For a meeting a new person:

I am always safe meeting a kind, compassionate woman or man who is compatible with me, having mutual grace, compassion, trust, love, peace and joy when healthy for me.

For jobs and money:

I am receiving and giving all the compatible jobs and money I want and need to take care of myself and _____ when healthy for me.

I am always safe and wealthy when healthy for me.

* *You may create and add more information to any of these messages.*

Ch. 4. Mysterious Gifts, p. 73 has details on how to focus on a pulse to aid in relaxation.

INSTRUCTIONS

I. Instructions for the Self-worth Exercise for yourself:

Fill in the Self-worth Excercise Sheet once a week
to see your progress.

Answer question # 1 with a number between "1 and 10."

Answer question no. 2 listing as many thoughts, feelings
and behavior you may have. The statements and questions
under no. 2 are to assist you to remember.

When your answer to question no. 1 is not 10, cross through
the number you wrote, and write "10." Now draw an arrow
from your new answer to the left hand column following no. 3.
This is your evidence for thinking, feeling and living that you
are 100% valuable because you have the gift of life.

Now draw an arrow from your answers in no. 2 to the right
hand column after no. 3. Now you can think and begin your
journey to feel you are 100% valuable, and you may also have
the above thoughts, feelings and behavior listed in no. 2. For
example: "I am 100% valuable, and I think or feel . . ." Also, you
now have a choice of changing your perspective (your thoughts
and feelings) about your answers listed in no. 2. Please write
your changes of thoughts, feelings, and behavior.

It is not uncommon for some people to see and understand
the logic of this reasoning, agree with it, and yet be unable to
feel these ideas in the beginning. As you persist with repetition
of this exercise, your thoughts, feelings and behavior may
follow. An example from everyday life is when you are learning
a new word. You may have experienced a period of time needed
while you are focusing on the meaning of a new word, as well
as using the new word before you feel the concept (meaning).

II. Instructions for Exercise for Others' Worth:

Use another sheet of paper and repeat this exercise answering the question "How valuable do you think or feel all people are, etc . . . ," and continue through no. 3.

III. Instructions for the Self-evaluation for Peace
and Inner Healing:

Fill in the Self-evaluation Work Sheet once a week to see your progress.

Read each statement focusing on "I" instead of "you, and all people." Circle the number that most describes how much you are doing these activities, rather than how much you believe these statements to be true. "1" (low) means you are not doing these activities very much. "7" (high) means you are doing these activities all the time. Do your best to answer intuitively and quickly.

After completing the page, write a comment on each of the statements, recording what you think and feel about each one. Using the principles of this healing method, change each statement to a healthy comfortable thought, and then in time your comfortable feelings and behavior (actions) may follow.

SELF-WORTH EXERCISE

(Discover and Release Mental/Emotional Traps)

1. How valuable did you think or feel you were when a situation went in a different direction than expected; when you may not have felt accepted or accepting; when you may have thought or felt you hadn't accomplished what you would have liked; and when you or others may not have thought, felt, or acted constructively?

    1=low, 10=high _____

2. If you did not answer 10, list your reasons why you did not:

    a. I thought and felt I was not 100% valuable because . . .

    b. I thought and felt I was not good enough because . . .

    c. What negative thoughts and feelings came to your mind?

    d. What did I think and feel I needed to be (or to have) to be valuable?

3. The following are evidences of how we are all 100% valuable because we have the gift of life:

On the one hand, remember that
the meaning of Universal Grace
is compassion, forgiveness, mercy,
and unmerited love.

On the other, hand
I thought and/or felt
the above.

Remember when you received
a blessing or opportunity.

What we do in life is
how we enjoy and take care
of ourselves and others.

Remember all of nature.
Nature is valuable
because it exists.

Remember when a new baby is
born, or when you may have lost
someone you loved.
You valued them because they existed.

Everyone is valuable, whether well or ill.

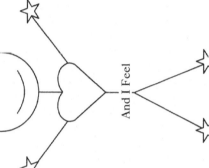

And I Feel

WE ARE ALWAYS SAFE NOT HURTING OURSELVES, YOU, OR OTHERS WHEN HEALTHY FOR US.

4. Write down one or more experiences of when you received an opportunity or blessing. These are some of your evidence that you are valuable just because you exist (—Because you are created, you are valuable).

when healthy for me.

5. Who do you want to be? I am a . . .

when healthy for me.

6. How do you want to be treated (by yourself and others)? I am always safe being treated with dignity, respect . . .

when healthy for me.

7. How do you want to treat others? I am always safe treating others with dignity, respect . . .

when healthy for us.

8. What do you want to think, feel and do that is healthy and enjoyable for you? I am safe (thinking, feeling, and doing . . .

when healthy for me.

9. What kind of healthy relationships do you want? How do you want to transform the relationships that you have? I am always safe enjoying a kind, considerate . . .

when healthy for me.

I, my family, friends, and business associates are always safe enjoying mutual grace, (what kind of relationship) . . .

when healthy for us.

10. Forming new relationships: I am always safe meeting a kind, considerate . . .

when healthy for me.

11. Are you handling money wisely? I am always safe wisely earning, saving, spending (receiving and giving) all the money I want and need to support myself and _____ . . .

when healthy for me or us.

12. How is your creativity and job? I am always safe receiving and giving all the creativity, talents, and enjoyable jobs I want and need to support myself, and _____ . . .

when healthy for me or us.

WE ARE ALWAYS SAFE BEING TOGETHER WHEN HEALTHY FOR US

SELF-EVALUATION FOR PEACE AND INNER HEALING

Circle
Low High

1. I am, you, and all people are always safe learning, knowing, and living truth when healthy for us.   1 2 3 4 5 6 7

2. I am always safe not hurting myself when healthy for me.   1 2 3 4 5 6 7

3. I am always safe not hurting others when healthy for me.   1 2 3 4 5 6 7

4. I am, you, and all people are always safe living and being wise when healthy for us.   1 2 3 4 5 6 7

5. I am, you, and all people are always safe asking questions when healthy for us.   1 2 3 4 5 6 7

6. I am, you, and all people are always safe when healthy for us.   1 2 3 4 5 6 7

7. I am, you, and all people are always safe, valuable, and cared for because we have the gift of life.

1 2 3 4 5 6 7

8. I am always safe letting go of fear, pain, guilt and punishment when healthy for me.

1 2 3 4 5 6 7

9. I am always safe letting go of anger when healthy for me.

1 2 3 4 5 6 7

10. I am always safe letting go of sadness when healthy for me.

1 2 3 4 5 6 7

11. I am always safe letting go of frustration when healthy for me.

1 2 3 4 5 6 7

12. I am always safe letting go of helplessness when healthy for me.

1 2 3 4 5 6 7

13. I am always safe letting go of worry when healthy for me.

1 2 3 4 5 6 7

14. I am always safe letting go of loneliness when healthy for me.

1 2 3 4 5 6 7

15. I am always safe not blaming or judging myself when healthy for me.

1 2 3 4 5 6 7

16. I am always safe not blaming or judging my family, friends, and all people when healthy for me.

1 2 3 4 5 6 7

17. I am always safe forgiving myself when healthy for me.

1 2 3 4 5 6 7

18. I am always safe forgiving my family, friends, and all people when healthy for me.

1 2 3 4 5 6 7

19. I am always safe thinking, feeling, and expressing myself when healthy for me.

1 2 3 4 5 6 7

20. I am always safe doing what I want when healthy for me.

1 2 3 4 5 6 7

21. I am always safe about the passing on of our loved ones and myself when healthy for me.

1 2 3 4 5 6 7

22. We are always safe talking and listening to ourselves, you, and all people when healthy for us.

1 2 3 4 5 6 7

23. We are always safe sharing when we feel uncomfortable or concern when healthy for us.

1 2 3 4 5 6 7

24. We are always safe listening and following our healthy inner voice.

1 2 3 4 5 6 7

25. We are always safe eating and drinking slowly what is healthy for us.

1 2 3 4 5 6 7

26. We are always safe receiving, saving, spending, and giving money when healthy for us.

1 2 3 4 5 6 7

27. We are always safe sleeping peacefully when healthy for us.

1 2 3 4 5 6 7

28. We are always safe balancing our time with ourselves, others, diet, rest, exercise, work, and play each day.
1 2 3 4 5 6 7

29. We are always safe being patient with ourselves when healthy for us.
1 2 3 4 5 6 7

30. We are always safe being patient with our family, friends, and all people when healthy for us.
1 2 3 4 5 6 7

31. We are always safe being understanding and thankful for ourselves, family, friends, and all people.
1 2 3 4 5 6 7

32. We are always safe enjoying an intimate relationship when healthy for us.
1 2 3 4 5 6 7

33. We are always safe receiving and giving grace, compassion, love, and peace to ourselves, you and 33. all people.
1 2 3 4 5 6 7

PEACE AND INNER HEALING

I am always safe learning, knowing, and living truth when healthy for me.

I am always safe living, and being wise when healthy for me.

I am always safe not hurting myself, you, or others when healthy for me.

We are always safe, valuable and cared for because we have the gift of life.

I am always safe letting go of fear, pain, guilt, and punishment when healthy for me.

We are always safe receiving and giving grace, compassion, love, and peace to ourselves, you, and all people when healthy for us.

We are always safe and healed when healthy for us.